DWELLING IN THE
SECRET PLACE

A Call to Intimacy With God

DEBBIE FLETCHER

Published by:

Editor: Cleveland O. McLeish (Author C. Orville McLeish)

ISBN: 978-1-965635-32-2 (Paperback)

ENDORSEMENT

In a time when fear and uncertainty threaten to cloud our faith, Pastor Debbie Fletcher offers a timely and powerful call back to the heart of God. Rooted in the timeless promises of Psalm 91, this book is a soul-stirring invitation for believers to dwell in the secret place and experience God's peace, protection, and presence like never before. With clarity, compassion, and deep spiritual insight, Fletcher encourages Christians to move beyond surface-level belief and into an unshakable, intimate relationship with God. This is not just a book—it's a journey into trust, refuge, and divine assurance. This is a must-read for every believer seeking to deepen their walk with God.

Mark Titus

Founder—Kingdom Sound Radio International

DEDICATION

This book is dedicated to all of God's people who have a desire to deepen their walk with Christ and to allow the Holy Spirit to be their teacher and guide throughout their spiritual journey. Additionally, this book is for anyone who is willing to embrace biblical principles and submit to the spiritual disciplines using it as a road map to a successful and productive life. I welcome you to the Secret Place.

ACKNOWLEDGMENTS

All praise, honour and glory go to my heavenly Father, for whose blessings, both naturally and spiritually, I am eternally grateful.

To my spiritual mother and first pastor, Pearline Lawrence, I love you dearly. Thank you for showing me the way into the secret place.

To Bishop Dr. Clayton Martin and his wife, Dr. Sonia Martin, thank you for your invaluable contribution to my spiritual growth and development in the Lord. Min. Martin, I recall with fond memories your Sunday School and Bible classes. Wow!

To my pastor, Colin Cole (deceased) and his wife, Pastor Valrie Vivienne Cole, your exemplary stewardship in the kingdom of God is beyond words. I am eternally indebted to you. Pastor Valrie, you make pastoral work enjoyable and taught me how to love in spite of and forgive without reservation.

To my immediate family, Stephen Fletcher, my husband of forty-two years, I love you dearly; my children, Dr. Bunny-Ann (Simone) Fletcher, Minister Jerann Williams (Delano), and my "Washie" Morris Williams, except for God, there would be no me without you. Thanks a million.

To my covenant friends, Derrick Cornwall, Doreen Williams, Janet Truth, Sophia Headley-Hunt, and the initial prayer group in Cayman, I thank you for the times spent in the secret place.

To everyone who has helped me along the way, this book is sincerely dedicated to you. Thank you.

FOREWORD

I am pleased to endorse and lend support to my fellow co-labourer in ministry, Debbie Fletcher, on the publication of her debut book "Dwelling in the Secret Place." Debbie has been known over the years for her passionate engagement with God in prayer, and it is no great wonder that her first book is representative of this level of engagement with God.

There is a definite pull to see what she sees and feel what she feels in pursuit of this most ultimate of all intimate connections. You are left with the realisation that this must be the epitome of all spiritual experiences that a human being can have with their Creator. As you pour through the content of these pages, you are left to meditate in awe concerning the love that God has for us in His provision of such a powerful and spiritual experience. This is definitely meant to fill the void in all humanity through this tangible call for dwelling in His presence. Her unique style of writing is captivating and makes you desire the experience rather than just be studious about the content.

The notion that the secret place is not fixed or confined to a physical location but is wherever we connect with God is both informative and revelatory. Reading this book allows us to glean from the careful analysis of scriptures and depth of thought that it is possible to have this treasured experience with God where individuals can connect with Him on a deeply personal level.

The use of discussion questions and a prayer at the end of the chapters only helps to deepen and make more meaningful the prayerful journey into intimacy with God. This book represents a clarion call for all believers to either renew their passion or continue this lifelong journey of intimacy with God, their Creator.

I believe that this book has whetted our appetites for more of God, and we expect more discourses from this author with the same level of bold conviction revealing the heart and mind of God for His people.

Bishop Valentine A. Rodney M.A., B.Sc.

Amazon Bestselling Author, Educator and Transformational Speaker

TABLE OF CONTENTS

INTRODUCTION

The concept of the secret place symbolizes a deeply personal and intimate connection with God through surrender, prayer, worship, and reflection. Within that space, believers experience God's presence, guidance, peace, and protection. Though the term "secret place" is not explicitly defined in scripture, its essence is vividly portrayed in passages like Psalm 91:1, *"He who dwells in the secret place of the Most High shall abide under the shadow of the Almighty" (NKJV)* and Psalm 15:1, *"Lord, who may abide in Your tabernacle? Who may dwell in Your holy hill?" (NKJV)*. Psalm 46:1, "God *is our refuge and strength, a very present help in trouble" (NKJV)*. This imagery highlights a spiritual refuge where believers can draw near to God, away from distractions, to seek His face and renew their strength.

In the Psalms, the "secret place" symbolizes a deep, intimate connection with God—a sanctuary of safety and divine protection. Amid the chaos of modern life, it is comforting to know that God offers a spiritual refuge not bound by physical location but hidden in His presence, waiting for believers to dwell in it. May this journey awaken your heart, refresh your spirit, and draw you closer to God.

In the book of Colossians, there is a reference to our lives being hidden with Christ in God, suggesting a spiritual connection between believers and God that is not always visible to the outside world. These references in the New Testament reinforce the idea that the secret place is a sacred space of communion, prayer, and inner connection with the divine, where one can find solace and spiritual nourishment. Therefore, it behoves us to pursue this sacred space with relentless audacity.

In the New Testament, Jesus alludes to the secret place in His teachings. In Matthew 6:6, He encourages His followers to go into their room, close the door, and pray to their Father in secret. This emphasizes the personal and private nature of one's relationship with God, who waits to hear us and answer our requests and petitions. Jesus refers to interaction within this space as a time of intimate communion with God. In His discourse, we see Him teaching His disciples and, by extension, the body of Christ the importance of secret prayer and interaction with the heavenly Father, stating that our heavenly Father sees us in secret and that He will reward us openly. Our approach to prayer should be with sincerity and humility.

First, He cautions against praying for public display, where the focus shifts from connecting with God to seeking human approval: *"When you pray, do not be like the hypocrites, for they love to pray standing in the synagogues and on the street corners to be seen by others" (Matthew 6:5 - AMPC).* Though outwardly impressive, such prayers lack genuine heart and miss the purpose of communing with God. On the other hand, prayers that are straightforward, heartfelt, and genuine are the ones that truly capture God's attention. We approach God with humility and authenticity, free from pretence or elaborate words, and our prayers resonate deeply with Him. It is not about the complexity of our language or the length of our petitions but rather the sincerity of our hearts and the faith behind our words. Simple prayers, offered with pure intentions and a trusting spirit, demonstrate our reliance on God and our recognition of His sovereignty. These are the prayers that reach His ears and touch His heart, as they reflect a genuine connection and a true desire to communicate with Him.

In successive chapters, repetition will be made concerning the secret place and those who seek to dwell within that intimate space; for example, the secret place is not confined to a physical location, though it is often described in such terms. Therefore, while references may point to physical spaces—like a quiet room, a secluded garden, or a private corner—the true essence of the secret place transcends the material world. It is primarily a spiritual posture of intimacy and connection with God, where believers retreat to pray, worship, and seek His presence.

CHAPTER 1

DWELLERS VERSUS VISITORS

There is a distinct difference between dwelling in a secret place and merely visiting it. Visiting the secret place implies occasional moments of prayer, worship, or meditation—it refers to a time when we seek God's presence during specific needs or challenges. These interactions can be deeply rewarding because they provide comfort, guidance, and renewal. However, dwelling in the secret place goes beyond sporadic visits; it should be a lifestyle of abiding in God's presence, where our hearts remain consistently connected to Him.

Persons who dwell in the secret place are more equipped to deal with the onslaughts of the enemy, and this kind of stability is what distinguishes David, the shepherd boy, from the other trained military soldiers in Saul's army. David was not only a shepherd caring for his sheep, but he was a worshipper. One gets the idea that most of his time was spent communicating with the good shepherd who prepared him for life's challenges. David ran confidently to the battle and faced Goliath while the Israelite soldiers ran away from

Goliath in fear. Are you running away from your Goliaths? Are you afraid of them? Learn from our brother David and build your confidence. He spent time with God in the secret place.

"But David said to Saul, let no man's heart fail because of him; thy servant will go and fight with this Philistine.' And Saul said to David, thou art not able to go against this Philistine to fight with him: for thou art but a youth, and he a man of war from his youth. And David said unto Saul, thy servant kept his father's sheep, and there came a lion and a bear, and took a lamb out of the flock: And I went out after him, and smote him, and delivered it out of his mouth: and when he arose against me, I caught him by his beard, and smote him, and slew him. Thy servant slew both the lion and the bear: and this uncircumcised Philistine shall be as one of them, seeing he hath defied the armies of the living God. David said moreover, The Lord that delivered me out of the paw of the lion, and out of the paw of the bear, he will deliver me out of the hand of this Philistine. And Saul said unto David, Go, and the Lord be with thee" (1 Samuel 17:32-37 NKJV).

To "dwell with" someone means to live or reside in close proximity to them. It implies a shared living space or a deep and intimate connection with another person. Dwelling with someone suggests a sense of coexistence, where individuals cohabit in harmony, support one another, and share their lives daily. It often involves building a home or a life together, fostering a sense of closeness, and creating a

18

foundation of mutual understanding, trust, and companionship.

The writer of Psalm 91 speaks from a place of intimacy and foreknowledge. It is evident that he has made this sacred space his abode and undoubtedly enjoys the benefits and blessings that are enjoined. He therefore introduces us to the place and the one we will encounter in this sacred sanctuary. He introduces us to the Almighty God and His divine protection and provisions. Some Bible scholars posit that Moses is the author of this portion of the Psalms, and I am inclined to agree with the narrative. The way the Psalm is structured gives credence to someone who encountered God throughout the rough and scorching terrains of life, and despite the negatives, the writer discovered and enjoyed the secrets and intimacy associated with cohabiting in that sacred dimension, if you will.

A CALL TO THE SECRET PLACE

In Matthew 11:28-29, the Lord Jesus makes an appeal, *"Come unto me, all ye that labour and are heavy laden and I will give you rest. Take my yoke upon you and learn of me; for I am meek and lowly in heart: and ye shall find rest unto your souls" (KJV).* This can be considered a universal invitation extended to all to discover solace and relief from any burdensome circumstances or challenges they may be facing. It beckons individuals to find relief and rejuvenation, regardless of the nature of their struggles, whether physical, emotional, spiritual, or otherwise. This heartfelt call urges

19

everyone to seek refuge, offering a refuge where consolation and comfort can be found. It is an open embrace, inviting individuals to release their burdens and find tranquillity, providing a safe haven where one can find rest from the weariness of life's trials.

Life presents numerous challenges, and we sometimes feel overwhelmed as we strive to navigate them and seek resolutions. The truth is, we encounter various struggles along our journey, and it is natural to occasionally feel overwhelmed. In our pursuit of answers, we may sometimes feel a sense of hopelessness and despair. It is during these vulnerable moments that the enemy seeks to prey upon us, threatening our well-being and spiritual growth. Therefore, it is essential to exercise caution and remain alert to safeguard ourselves from succumbing to these cunning snares, so the invitation to "Come" should be heeded by all and approached with a sense of urgency and immediacy, requiring a prompt response. This call highlights the importance of not hesitating to accept the invitation. This call demands a swift and decisive reaction, recognizing the significance and urgency of the opportunity being presented. It urges individuals to prioritize and act promptly, understanding that the invitation holds great value and should not be postponed or taken lightly. The invitation unequivocally states that there are no exceptions or exclusions regarding who should respond to the call. It emphasizes that everyone will be warmly welcomed, thus encouraging everyone to attend, come and experience a place of calmness and renewal where you can find comfort and transformation—experience a haven of peace and restoration, where the burdens of life are lifted, and our heavenly Father is waiting to welcome us with open arms and a loving embrace. So, whether you are in a far country like the prodigal son, who left your father's home, or you are still at home like the elder brother who did not leave but was not in right standing, please know Daddy is waiting for you in the secret place.

Luke 15:18-20a, "I will arise and go to my father, and will say unto him, Father, I have sinned against heaven, and before thee, and am no more worthy to be called thy son: make me as one of thy hired servants. And he arose and came to his father" (KJV).

God knows that we cannot navigate life successfully without the assistance of divine help, which can only be found in Him. He knows our limitations and weaknesses; therefore, we must acknowledge our dependence on God, recognizing that He understands our journey and the need for His intervention. Psalm 91:1 assures us that those who live in the secret and hidden sanctuary of the Most High will find refuge under His protective care. So, let us acknowledge our dependence on God. Let us accept His invitation to dwell with Him in the secret place so we can establish a deep and intimate connection with Him.

The invitation needs to be answered quickly and without delay. It is important to respond promptly and not put it off. This means understanding the urgency and importance of the invitation and taking action right away rather than waiting. Jesus clearly states in the scripture, *"I am the way, the truth, and the life: no man cometh unto the Father, but by me. If ye had known me, ye should have known my father also: and from henceforth ye know him, and have seen him."* *(John 14:6-7 – KJV).* This revelation makes it clear that the only way to reach the Father is by accepting the Spirit's call to embrace Jesus' redemptive work on the cross. It shows that we cannot have a relationship with the Father unless we respond to the Holy Spirit's urging and believe in the forgiveness and salvation offered through Jesus' sacrifice. In simpler terms, it means we can only connect with God by accepting Jesus as our Saviour, as prompted by the Holy Spirit.

SUMMARY

The secret place is not confined to a physical location, but rather, it is a metaphorical one. It represents an inner sanctuary where believers can pour out their hearts, confess their sins, express their deepest desires, and listen for the voice of God. It is a place of vulnerability, honesty, and absolute surrender, where individuals can experience the outpouring of God's love, mercy, and forgiveness as we seek to cultivate a deeper intimacy with God and nurture our faith so we can develop and mature spiritually.

DISCUSSION QUESTIONS

Psalm 91:1 teaches, *"He who dwells in the secret place of the Most High shall abide under the shadow of the Almighty" (KJV).* What does it mean to dwell in the secret place of God, and how can one actively seek and maintain that closeness with God in our daily lives?

Dwelling in the secret place offers a profound sense of refuge, protection, and spiritual sustenance in God's presence. How does consistently abiding in this intimate space with Him transform the way we face fear, anxiety, and life's challenges, as illustrated in Psalm 91:2-4? What practical steps can we take to deepen our trust and reliance on God, ensuring that His presence becomes our anchor in every season of life?

In Psalm 27:4, David expresses his desire to *"dwell in the house of the Lord all the days of his life" (KJV).* How can we relate this longing for God's presence to the idea of dwelling in the secret place? What role do worship, prayer, and fellowship with other believers play in helping individuals dwell continually in God's presence, both in church settings and in their everyday lives?

PRAYER

Heavenly Father, we come before You with hearts full of gratitude, thanking You for the gracious invitation to enter into this sacred space where Your presence dwells. It is a profound honour to stand before You, the Creator of all things, and to be welcomed into Your divine presence. We acknowledge that You are holy, loving, and merciful, and we are humbled by the privilege of drawing near to You.

Thank you for the opportunity to lay our burdens, cares, and concerns before you. You know the depths of our hearts, the struggles we face, and the challenges that weigh heavily upon us. Father, we trust in your promise that when we come to you, we will find solace, comfort, and relief. Your Word assures us that you are our refuge and strength, a very present help in times of trouble (see Psalm 46:1). Father, help us to live by this truth, knowing that you are faithful to carry our burdens and provide peace that surpasses all understanding.

Today, Lord, we bring to you every circumstance that feels overwhelming, every challenge that seems insurmountable, and every worry that clouds our minds. We ask for your wisdom, guidance, and strength to navigate these difficulties. Help us to release our anxieties into your capable hands, trusting that you are working all things together for our good (see Romans 8:28). Father, cause us to find rest in the assurance that you are in control, even when life feels uncertain.

Father, thank you for the peace that comes from surrendering our lives to you. Teach us to rely not on our own understanding but to lean wholly on you, acknowledging you in all our ways (see Proverbs 3:5-6).

May your presence fill us with hope, courage, and confidence, knowing that you are with us every step of the way.

We praise you, Abba, for your unfailing love and faithfulness. Thank you for being our Comforter, Healer, and Provider. May we always remember that in You we find the strength to overcome, the grace to endure, and the joy to persevere.

Amen.

CHAPTER 2

ENTRANCE INTO THE SECRET PLACE

"Lord, who shall abide in thy tabernacle? Who shall dwell in thy holy hill? He that walketh uprightly, and worketh righteousness, and speaketh the truth in his heart. He that backbiteth not with his tongue, nor doeth evil to his neighbour, nor taketh up a reproach against his neighbour." *(Psalm 15:1-3 – KJV).*

Now that we know there is a special place where God lives, let us think about how we can enter that holy and important space. The scripture raises the question of who is qualified to dwell in God's presence and abide in His holy dwelling. It states that those who live uprightly, practice righteousness, and speak truthfully from their hearts are the ones who can dwell in God's tabernacle and holy hill. The question raised by the Psalmist was not rhetorical; it was answered unequivocally. However, this answer presents a challenge in today's theology, as many people hold the belief that they can live however they please and still maintain their relationship with God. However, a careful examination of Psalm 15:1-3 reveals that there exists a clear expectation and standard for those who seek to dwell in the presence of the Lord. It emphasizes the importance of refraining from gossip, avoiding harm to neighbours, and refusing to engage in any form of slander or reproach against persons. These negative qualities will keep us away from dwelling in God's holy presence.

These character traits present a challenge for all of us. The average person cannot achieve the opposite of these character traits unless they experience a spiritual transformation through being born again. Every person is born with a sinful nature, influenced by wrongdoing from the very beginning, and this is inherited because of Adam's act of disobedience.

Romans 5:19-21, "For as by one man's disobedience many were made sinners, so by the obedience of one shall many be made righteous. Moreover, the law entered, that the offence might abound. But where sin abounded, grace did much more abound: That as sin hath reigned unto death, even so, might grace reign through righteousness unto eternal life by Jesus Christ our Lord." (KJV).

The person who has not undergone transformation or remains unchanged possesses the ability to engage in actions associated with the flesh, as detailed in Galatians 5:19-21a, *"Now the works of the flesh are manifest, which are these; Adultery, fornication, uncleanness, lasciviousness, idolatry, witchcraft, hatred, variance, emulations, wrath, strife, seditions, heresies, envying, murders, drunkenness, revelling, and such like." (KJV).*

Consequently, the importance of receiving salvation by accepting the finished work of Jesus Christ on the cross of Calvary is a prerequisite for abiding in the secret place of the Most High.

THE ONLY WAY

Jesus is the door to a multiplicity of experiences with God; hence, our salvation experience is fundamental but not limited. Sadly, this initial experience is the only encounter that most of the Christian community enjoys because we simply never move from the door into the Father's kingdom. Imagine yourself invited to a large function with many guests and lots of food and entertainment were provided. Upon arrival, the host welcomed everyone and encouraged them to partake freely of what was provided because he prepared it with everyone in mind. But although you heard and accepted his generous and loving gesture, you went straight back to the door and stood there smiling and greeting others who were coming in. This candid imagery depicts the salvation experience for many believers; sadly, we are mere admirers of the things of God but never fully enjoyed it.

Jesus invites us to His Father's kingdom, but we are so mesmerized by what is happening at the entrance that we only enjoy it from the entrance while others pass us to actually partake of what is on the inside and beyond. I believe the time has come for us to move beyond the door into the storehouses—the banquet halls as it were—and collect the packages that are stored up for us, enjoy the meals that were provided and have fun.

"O the depth of the riches both of the wisdom and knowledge of God! how unsearchable are his judgments, and his ways past finding out!" (Romans 11:33 – KJV).

"Jesus saith unto him, I am the way, the truth, and the life: no man cometh unto the Father, but by me. If ye had known me, ye should have known my Father also: and from henceforth ye know him, and have seen him. Philip saith unto him, Lord, show us the Father, and it sufficeth us. Jesus saith unto him, have I been so long time with you, and yet hast thou not known me, Philip? He that hath seen me hath seen the Father; and how sayest thou then, Show us the Father? Believest thou not that I am in the Father, and the Father in me? The words that I speak unto you I speak not of myself: but the Father that dwelleth in me, he doeth the works." (John 14:6-10 - KJV).

This conversation between Jesus and Philip reveals that having a relationship with Jesus and listening to His teachings allows us to know and see the Father intimately. Jesus explains that He is the way, the truth, and the life, and no one can come to the Father except through Him. Philip asked to see the Father, but Jesus tells him that seeing Jesus is seeing the Father, as they are united. Jesus clarifies that

His words and actions are not from Himself but from the Father who dwells within Him.

Jesus is the way into the secret place. He is the one who was sent from God to both restore and return man to the secret place, the place where God dwells. Over the course of numerous centuries, humanity has relentlessly explored various avenues in their quest to establish a connection with the divine, often disregarding the recommended or designated approach and instead opting for their interpretations and innovations in the realm of spirituality and religious practice, which, in most cases, is to make a name for themselves as seen at the tower of Babel.

"They said to each other, "Come, let's make bricks and bake them thoroughly." They used brick instead of stone, and tar for mortar. Then they said, "Come, let us build ourselves a city, with a tower that reaches to the heavens, so that we may make a name for ourselves; otherwise, we will be scattered over the face of the whole earth." (Genesis 11:13 - NIV).

This innate human inclination towards experimentation and divergence from established norms is expressed through diverse cultural forms of worship and practices which are not scripturally entrenched. But sadly, in all this, man has failed miserably. Jeremiah 10:23 states, *"I know that the way of man is not in himself: it is not in man that walketh to direct his steps." (KJV).* Why? *"There is a way which seemeth right unto a man, but the end thereof is the ways of death." (Proverbs 14:12 - KJV).*

SUMMARY

Due to the inherent fallen nature of man and its persistent inclination to rebel against God's divine instructions and guidance, there exists a dire and ongoing risk of self-destruction unless individuals collectively and individually choose to respond and return to a harmonious relationship with their heavenly Father. But this can only be achieved if and when we accept the vicarious death of Jesus Christ.

DISCUSSION QUESTIONS

In John 10:9, Jesus declares, *"I am the door. If anyone enters by me, he will be saved and will go in and out and find pasture."* (*KJV*). How does Jesus serve as the entrance to the secret place in our relationship with God? What significance does this have for our salvation and spiritual journey?

Hebrews 10:19-20 says, *"Therefore, brothers and sisters, since we have the confidence to enter the Most Holy Place by the blood of Jesus, by a new and living way opened for us through the curtain, that is, His body."* (*ESV*). How does the shedding of Jesus' blood and His sacrifice on the cross pave the way for believers to enter the secret place of God's presence? What does this mean for our access to God and forgiveness of sins?

Jesus often withdrew to solitary places to pray and commune with God (see Luke 5:16). How can we follow Jesus' example in our own lives to enter into the secret place through prayer and intimacy with God? What role does faith in Jesus play in deepening our connection to God and experiencing the benefits of dwelling in the secret place?

PRAYER

Heavenly Father,
We come before you with hearts overflowing with gratitude and reverence, thanking You for the immeasurable gift of Your Son, Jesus Christ. Thank You for Your boundless love and mercy, demonstrated in sending Jesus into the world to redeem humanity. You saw our brokenness, sin, and need for a Saviour, and in Your infinite wisdom and grace, You provided the ultimate sacrifice to reconcile us to Yourself. Lord, we are forever humbled by this profound act of love.

Jesus, our Saviour and Redeemer, we thank You for willingly offering Yourself as the Lamb of God who takes away the sins of the world. You bore the weight of our transgressions, endured the cross, and triumphed over sin and death so we might have eternal life. Your sacrifice was not out of obligation but out of love—a love so deep and pure that it defies human understanding. Thank You for laying down Your life so we might be set free from the chains of sin and death.

Through Your precious sacrifice, Lord Jesus, we now have access to the throne of grace. What a profound and awe-inspiring privilege it is to approach the God of the universe with confidence, knowing that we are welcomed as beloved children. Your blood has cleansed us; Your righteousness has clothed us, and Your Spirit has empowered us to draw near to the Father without fear or shame. We are eternally grateful for this gift of reconciliation and intimacy with You.

Father, we ask that You help us never to take this incredible gift for granted. Please help us live each day in the light of Your grace, walking in the freedom and victory that Jesus secured for us. Teach us to approach Your throne of grace with boldness and humility, knowing that we can find mercy and grace to help us in our time of need (see Hebrews 4:16). May our lives reflect the depth of our gratitude for the salvation we have received.

Jesus, we honour You as our Saviour, King, and Friend. Thank You for making a way where there seemed to be no way. Thank You for bridging the gap between humanity and divinity, for tearing the veil, and for inviting us into a relationship with the Father. By His grace and mercy, we will live each day in awe of Your sacrifice and the joy of Your resurrection.

Amen.

CHAPTER 3

FIRST DWELLERS

The first man, Adam, and his wife, Eve, enjoyed a sacred space of communion and fellowship with God prior to the fall. He and his wife were in a realm of inconceivable glory and sinless perfection until the day they sinned by disobeying God's instruction to not eat from the Tree of Knowledge of Good and Evil. Subsequently, they were judged for their wrongdoing and driven from the garden, and an angel with a flaming sword was placed at the entrance of the garden.

Genesis 3:24, "And he placed at the east of the Garden of Eden a Cherub and a flaming sword which turned to guard the way to the tree of life" (NIV).

This severe action from God speaks to His absolute intolerance for sinful practices and blatant disregard for authority. God is infinitely holy, and where He dwells is holy. Therefore, whoever chooses to dwell with Him must meet the criteria: be ye holy, for God is holy. Holiness, in this context, connotes respect, reverence, and absolute obedience. When we speak of holiness, we refer to a sacred state of being marked by a profound respect for God's commandments and a steadfast commitment to following His divine guidance. In this light, it is indeed a poignant thought that the act of banishing Adam and Eve from paradise would have pained the heart of God.

The expulsion of the first man and woman from the Garden of Eden was a consequence of their disobedience and violation of God's explicit commandment. This act, while necessary due to their transgression, can reflect God's justice and commitment to upholding the sanctity of His divine decrees. Yet, it is also a moment that signifies human separation from the closeness and intimacy with God that was once enjoyed in the paradise of Eden.

Imagine the heart of God, full of love and compassion, watching as His beloved creations face the consequences of their actions. While the expulsion was a just response to disobedience, it was a painful separation that must have evoked a sense of grief in a loving God who enjoys intimacy and communion with His children. It highlights the complex relationship between God's justice and His love for His children, underscoring the profound depth of His emotions and the intricate relationship between holiness, obedience, and the human experience.

The Garden of Eden housed a secret sanctuary where Adam and his wife, Eve, could interact intimately with God. The same is true for everyone who seeks to dwell with the Lord in the secret place; we too will enjoy uninterrupted times of intense fellowship with our Creator. However, we should not ignore the traps and snares of the enemy of our souls as he relentlessly seeks to intrude and disrupt our communication and fellowship with God.

John 10:10, "The thief comes only in order to steal and kill and destroy. I came that they may have and enjoy life, and have it in abundance to the full, till it overflows." (AMPC).

It is the enemy's intention to interfere with our flow. To interrupt the flow refers to the act of disrupting or obstructing the smooth and uninterrupted progression of something in the context of our communication and fellowship with God. It implies that the interference or disturbance caused by external factors, such as lack of motivation and discouragement, are caused by the enemy of our soul, the chief agent of destabilization and frustration. These disruptions can manifest in various ways, such as doubts, temptations, distractions, or negative influences that hinder our connection with God.

The goal of the enemy is to create obstacles and divert our attention away from maintaining a deep and meaningful relationship with God. As a result, recognizing and overcoming these interruptions is crucial to preserve and nurture our spiritual connection so that we remain in the secret place with God.

In the Garden of Eden, Adam and Eve thrived in abundant wealth, well-being, and delight, and it was a beautiful and delightful atmosphere—simply put, one that would take your breath away, as the proverbial statement implies. However, this harmonious state was abruptly disrupted by the intrusion of the enemy, causing a disturbance in the once seamless flow of blessings and tranquillity. The man and his wife went from enjoying intimacy and fellowship with God in the cool of the day to hiding from God among the trees (see Genesis 3:7-13). The enemy's interference brought about a shift from a peaceful existence to a state of turmoil, introducing strife, doubt, and the potential for separation from the original intended communion with God. The interruption by the enemy shattered the perfect equilibrium that they once enjoyed, prompting the need for redemption and restoration to regain the lost harmony. Hence, the revealing of man's attempt to redeem himself by using fig leaves and the introduction of the blood sacrifice prefigures man's redemption through the death, burial, and resurrection of Jesus Christ.

Hebrews 10:4-6, "For it is not possible that the blood of bulls and of goats should take away sins. Wherefore when he cometh into the world, he saith, Sacrifice and offering thou wouldest not, but a body hast thou prepared me: In burnt offerings and sacrifices for sin thou hast had no pleasure." (KJV).

SUMMARY

The way into the secret place is a correct understanding of truth as it relates to where the secret place is located and who gets to live there. Access to the secret place is not attained through adherence to a set of traditions or man-made rules but rather by embracing and following the teachings and instructions of Christ. It is not about conforming to external rituals or regulations but about aligning one's heart, mind, and actions with the profound wisdom and guidance found in the Word of God. The key lies in embracing the transformative power of His teachings, embodying His love and grace, and surrendering to His divine authority. Through this intimate connection with Christ and His teachings, one discovers the path to the secret place, where communion with God is experienced in its fullest depth and authenticity. God, the Father, provides this space for interaction and relationship with His children.

The place of intimacy and relationship was severed and destroyed by sin. However, God prepared a way for restoration and communion with His children. This place is called the "Secret Place." You are cordially invited into the secret place where Father God is waiting to welcome you.

God wants to restore broken relationships, so if your relationship with God is affected by sin and you are struggling to regain your relationship with Him, I recommend repentance and submission to His Word.

INVITATION

If you have never experienced a relationship with God, you might have wondered, "Is it even possible for me to have a connection with this God?" Based on what you have heard about Him, it may appear as though He would never accept someone like you. Perhaps you carry the weight of past mistakes, having done some terrible things or messed up significantly. However, it is essential to reframe these thoughts. Despite your shortcomings and missteps, it is indeed possible to forge a relationship with God. His unfathomable love and mercy extend to all, offering forgiveness, redemption, and a fresh start. No matter your past, God is eager to embrace you with open arms.

DISCUSSION QUESTIONS

How does the communion between Adam, Eve, and God in the Garden of Eden shape our understanding of their relationship with the divine, and what lessons can we draw from this relationship for our spiritual lives today?

The Garden of Eden narrative emphasizes the loss of communion between Adam, Eve, and God after their disobedience. How does the theme of separation from God in this story resonate with the human experience of spiritual longing and the search for reconciliation with the deity in different cultures and religions throughout history?

What factors or influences do you think played a role in Adam and Eve succumbing to evil and disobedience in the Garden of Eden? Please elaborate on the circumstances or motivations that might have contributed to this significant event in the biblical narrative.

PRAYER

Heavenly Father,
I come before You with a heart full of humility and honesty, acknowledging my position as a sinner. I recognize that sin entered the world through the disobedience of Adam and Eve, and because of this, I, too, have fallen short of Your glory. I confess that I have not lived up to Your perfect standards, and I am deeply aware of my need for Your mercy and grace. Yet, even in my brokenness, I am reminded of Your boundless love and compassion.

Thank You, Father, for not condemning me in my sin but instead offering me the incredible opportunity to come into a right relationship with You. Your love is so vast that You provided a way for me to be reconciled to You through the sacrifice of Your Son, Jesus Christ. I am in awe of Your kindness and patience as You continually call me to turn away from my sin and embrace the new life You offer.

Lord, I ask for Your help to fully accept this invitation of grace. Open my heart to receive the forgiveness and transformation only You can provide. Help me to surrender my pride, doubts, and fears, and to trust in Your promise that if I confess my sins, You are faithful and just to forgive me and cleanse me from all unrighteousness (see 1 John 1:9). I long to be made new in Christ, to be transformed by the renewing of my mind, and to walk in the freedom and purpose You have prepared for me.

Father, I pray that You will strengthen my faith and deepen my understanding of Your love. Help me to fully grasp the depth of what it means to be forgiven and restored by You. May I live each day in gratitude for the gift of salvation, and may my life be a reflection of Your grace and mercy to others.

Thank You for not giving up on me, pursuing me with Your love, and offering me a fresh start. I surrender my life to You, Lord, and I ask that You would guide me into a deeper, more intimate relationship with You. Please help me walk in obedience to Your Word so Your name will be glorified.

CHAPTER 4

THE WRITTEN WORD

The scripture holds the ultimate authority in spiritual matters and uses various metaphors to highlight that Jesus is the exclusive path to the Father. It depicts Jesus as the door to the sheepfold and the true vine, with His Father as the caretaker of the vineyard while we, the believers, are the branches.

"Verily, verily, I say unto you, He that entereth not by the door into the sheepfold, but climbeth up some other way, the same is a thief and a robber. But he that entereth in by the door is the shepherd of the sheep." (John 10:1-2 - KJV).

"I am the true vine, and my Father is the husbandman. Every branch in me that beareth not fruit he taketh away: and every branch that beareth fruit, he purgeth it, that it may bring forth more fruit. Now ye are clean through the word which I have spoken unto you. Abide in me, and I in you. As the branch cannot bear fruit of itself, except it abide in the vine; no more can ye, except ye abide in me. I am the vine, ye are the branches: He that abideth in me, and I in him, the

same bringeth forth much fruit: for without me ye can do nothing. If a man abides not in me, he is cast forth as a branch, and is withered; and men gather them, and cast them into the fire, and they are burned. If ye abide in me, and my words abide in you, ye shall ask what ye will, and it shall be done unto you." (John 15:1-7 - KJV).

These metaphors emphasize a deep interconnectedness and relationship involving three aspects: Jesus, the Father, and us. Through these metaphors, it becomes clear that our connection to the Father is solely through Jesus, and our relationship with Him is intricately intertwined, just like branches to a vine or sheep to a fold. Therefore, in order to ensure a proper connection with our heavenly Father, we must follow the guidance of the scripture. Jesus is the pathway to the Father.

"I am the door: by me if any man enter in, he shall be saved, and shall go in and out, and find pasture. The thief cometh not, but for to steal, and to kill, and to destroy: I am come that they might have life, and that they might have it more abundantly." (John 10:9-10 – KJV).

Therefore, by adhering to the teachings of the scripture and recognizing Jesus as the way, we can maintain a correct and meaningful relationship with our heavenly Father; by embracing the teachings and guidance found within the scriptures, we open ourselves to the rich and transformative experiences that come from connecting with God through His Son, Jesus Christ.

During earthly ministry, Jesus was frequently faced with opposition from the Pharisees, particularly when He assumed divine authority. Their responses were marked by strong indignation, and there were instances where they even plotted to take His life.

"Jesus answered them, Many good works have I shewed you from my Father; for which of those works do you stone me? The Jews answered him, saying, for a good work we stone thee not; but for blasphemy; and because that thou, being a man, makest thyself God." (John 10:32-33 – KJV).

Jesus provides the pathway to a variety of meaningful experiences with our heavenly Father within a sacred space. However, in order to have these encounters, we need to willingly submit ourselves to the authority of the scriptures. The instruction is obvious:

"Search the scriptures; for in them ye think ye have eternal life: and they are they which testify of me." (John 5:39 - KJV).

The Word of God serves as our invaluable guide and navigational tool, leading us into the depths of divine truth. It serves as a comprehensive search engine, aiding us in our quest for spiritual enlightenment and understanding. Its wisdom and teachings illuminate our path, ensuring we stay on course as we explore the realms of profound spiritual knowledge. Apostle Paul writes in Romans 11:33, *"Oh, the depth of the riches and wisdom and knowledge of God! How unsearchable are His judgments and decisions and how unfathomable and untraceable are His ways!" (AMP).*

As we approach the rich treasury of the scripture, let us do so with an open heart and a desire to encounter God's truth because this will lead us into the secret place. Say like the Psalmist, *"Open thou mine eyes that I may behold wondrous things out of thy law" (Psalm 119:18 - ESV).* These words from the psalmist encapsulate a heartfelt plea to God, seeking illumination and understanding of the profound truths contained within His law.

"With my whole heart have I sought thee: O let me not wander from thy commandments. Thy word have I hid in mine heart, that I might not sin against thee." (Psalm 119:10-11 – KJV).

Indeed, the Bible is full of wondrous things, unveiling deep truths that can guide, inspire, and transform our existence. Its narratives, teachings, and prophecies provide profound insights into the human condition, God's nature, and our existence and purpose. Amidst the vast array of wondrous things in the Bible, the one that stands above all is the immeasurable love God demonstrated for humanity. The depths and breadth of God's love surpass human comprehension. It is a love that transcends time, extends to every corner of the world, and embraces every individual. God's love is unconditional, unmerited, and unfathomable. It knows no bounds, surpassing our understanding and permeating every aspect of our lives. The writer of the old hymn, "The Love of God," captures the essence of this love and beautifully expressed it: "this love" that God has for us surpasses any human capacity to articulate or convey with words. Its magnitude and depth go beyond what language or writing instruments can ever hope to capture. The song states:

The love of God is greater far
Than tongue or pen can ever tell;
It goes beyond the highest star,
And reaches to the lowest hell;
The guilty pair, bowed down with care,
God gave His Son to win;
His erring child He reconciled,
And pardoned from his sin.

God's love is further demonstrated through the gift of His Son for the salvation of all.

"For God so loved the world, that He gave His only begotten Son, that whosoever believeth in Him should not perish, but have everlasting life. For God sent not his Son into the world to condemn the world; but that the world through Him might be saved." (John 3:16-17 – KJV).

To experience God's love is the most wonderful thing any human being can ever possess. It brings solace to the broken-hearted, healing to the wounded, and hope to the despairing. God's love extends forgiveness to the repentant, grace to the undeserving, and redemption to the lost. Essentially, God's love reconciles, restores, and transforms lives. Furthermore, in the face of adversity, God's love remains steadfast, providing strength, comfort, and an unshakeable foundation.

So, as we immerse ourselves in the holy scriptures, may our eyes be opened to behold the wondrous things that are contained therein, and may we be captivated by the magnitude of God's love. Let us draw from the depth of its richness and allow His love to permeate every facet of our being.

As we study God's Word, seeking to understand and apply it to our lives, we will experience divine revelation and insight that will lead us into a deeper and more intimate relationship with Him. Jesus' dialogue with the Pharisees reveals a profound truth that should guide all who desire to understand and personally know God. The Pharisees were instructed to examine the scriptures as they bear witness to the essence of Jesus' identity. Jesus told them to thoroughly search and explore the scriptures, for within its pages, they would discover a compelling testimony revealing the very essence and true nature of Jesus (see John. 5:39).

The Word of God holds ultimate authority in all matters pertaining to God, encompassing the past, present, and future. Within the Bible, we find the mind and will of God, serving as a guide for our lives. It is a divine revelation that provides insight into God's character; His plans and desires for humanity.

"For I know the plans I have for you, declares the LORD, plans to prosper you and not to harm you, plans to give you hope and a future." (Jeremiah 29:11 - NIV).

Through the pages of the Bible, we gain wisdom and understanding, discovering the principles and teachings that shape our relationship with God and one another. The Word of God speaks to us personally, addressing our spiritual needs, offering comfort in times of distress, and providing direction in moments of uncertainty. It is a timeless source of truth that remains relevant and applicable to our lives today.

"There are many plans in a man's heart, nevertheless the LORD's counsel—that will stand." (Proverbs 19:21 – NKJV).

As we embrace the truths found in the Word of God as our ultimate authority, we will discover the path to living a life that honours and reflects His divine will, bringing fulfilment and eternal significance to our existence.

"Thou wilt show me the path of life: in thy presence is fullness of joy; at thy right hand there are pleasures for evermore." (Psalm 16:11 – KJV).

This profound statement in the Psalms beautifully portrays the essence of a life lived in union with Christ. It reveals a divine invitation to walk a path of life guided by God's loving presence, where He becomes our steadfast refuge and offers us security and assurance. It signifies a journey of purpose, fulfilment, and protection, where God reveals His will, directs our steps, and grants us the joy and abundant life found in Him.

SUMMARY

Since the Word of God serves as a guide or blueprint into the secret place, I encourage each of us to diligently search the scriptures. Within its pages, we encounter Jesus—the one who stands as the door, the gateway to eternal life. In our quest, let us approach the scriptures with open hearts and minds, seeking the profound truths and revelations they hold. Additionally, we will discover the wondrous testimonies and prophecies that foretold the coming of the Messiah, pointing to Jesus as the fulfilment of God's promises. Let us consider this passage:

"In the beginning was the Word, and the Word was with God, and the Word was God. The same was in the beginning with God. All things were made by him; and without him was not anything made that was made. In him was life; and the life was the light of men." (John 1:1-4 – KJV).

Through Him, we find forgiveness, redemption, and the pathway to eternal life. Jesus, the embodiment of grace and truth, offers us the key to an everlasting relationship with God. Through faith in Him, we enter into a vibrant and intimate connection with our Creator, experiencing the fullness of life that transcends the temporal and reaches into eternity. So let us diligently search the scriptures, for within their pages we encounter the living Word, Jesus Christ, who invites us to walk through the door of eternal life and partake in the abundant blessings that He offers to all who believe in Him.

DISCUSSION QUESTIONS

Psalm 119:105 declares, *"Your word is a lamp for my feet and a light on my path" (KJV)*.

How does the use of scripture serve as a guiding light for believers seeking to remain connected with God in their secret place of prayer and devotion? What practical strategies can individuals employ to incorporate scripture into their daily time with God?

In Matthew 4:4, Jesus said, *"Man shall not live by bread alone, but by every word that comes from the mouth of God"* (KJV). How does this statement by Jesus emphasize the vital role of scripture in our spiritual nourishment and connection with God? How can regularly meditating on and applying God's Word strengthen one's relationship with Him in the secret place?

Apostle Paul encourages believers to *"Let the word of Christ dwell in you richly"* in Colossians 3:16. How does immersing ourselves in scripture impact our ability to remain connected with God in the secret place? What are some practical benefits and challenges of incorporating

God's Word into our daily spiritual practices, and how can we overcome these challenges?

PRAYER

Heavenly Father,

I ask that each time I come before You and draw near to Your Word, please help me to approach with a heart full of reverence and humility. Please help me to recognize that Your Word is not merely ink on paper but a living, breathing revelation of who You are—a divine invitation to know You more deeply. I humbly ask for Your guidance each time I open these pages, for I know that without Your Spirit to illuminate my understanding, I cannot fully grasp the depth of Your truth.

Lord, I surrender my will and intellect to You. Help me set aside my preconceptions, distractions, and limited understanding. Teach me to approach Your Word not as a passive reader but as an eager learner, ready to receive what You desire to reveal. Quiet my heart and mind so I may truly hear Your voice and comprehend the profound truths You are unveiling about Yourself. Let this time in Your Word be more than an exercise; let it be a sacred encounter with You, the Author of all wisdom and truth.

Each time I open Your Word or listen to Your Word being read, cause my heart to be open, receptive, and yielded to Your divine wisdom.

Heavenly Father, I acknowledge that Your thoughts are higher than my thoughts, and Your ways are beyond my understanding (see Isaiah 55:9). So, I trust that through Your Word, You will reveal Yourself to me in ways that transform my mind, renew my spirit, and draw me closer to You.

Please, let Your truth penetrate the deepest parts of my being, reshaping my perspective, refining my character, and aligning my desires with Yours.

Father, I invite Your divine presence to fill this space in this moment. Illuminate my mind and heart with the light of Your truth. Let Your Word come alive in me, not just as knowledge but as a living, active force that transforms me from the inside out. May it challenge, comfort, and compel me to walk in greater obedience and faith. Draw me closer to the essence of who You are—the God of love, justice, mercy, and holiness.

Father, I long for this time in Your Word to be more than a routine; I desire it to be a transformative encounter that deepens my relationship with You. May Your Spirit guide me into all truth (see John 16:13), and may Your Word become a lamp to my feet and a light to my path (see Psalm 119:105). Let it shape my thoughts, actions, and life so that I may reflect Your glory in all I do.

Amen.

CHAPTER 5

CONFIDENTLY ABIDING

"I am the true vine, and my Father is the husbandman. Every branch in me that beareth not fruit He taketh away: and every branch that beareth fruit, He purgeth it, that it may bring forth more fruit. Now ye are clean through the word which I have spoken unto you. Abide in me, and I in you. As the branch cannot bear fruit of itself, except it abide in the vine; no more can ye, except ye abide in Me. I am the vine, ye are the branches: He that abideth in me, and I in him, the same bringeth forth much fruit: for without Me ye can do nothing. If a man abides not in me, he is cast forth as a branch, and is withered; and men gather them, and cast them into the fire, and they are burned. If ye abide in me, and my words abide in you, ye shall ask what ye will, and it shall be done unto you. Herein is my Father glorified, that ye bear much fruit; so shall ye be my disciple." (John 15:1-8 – KJV).

"Confidently" implies that someone is expressing or demonstrating a strong belief or assurance in something. When a person acts confidently, they typically do so with a sense of self-assuredness, conviction, and certainty in their actions, decisions, or statements. Confidence often suggests that the individual believes in their abilities, knowledge, or opinions and is not hesitant or unsure. It can also convey a sense of trustworthiness and reliability in the context of their actions or words. In essence, when someone acts confidently, they are indicating that they have faith in what they are doing or saying. So, to say we are confidently abiding in Jesus Christ is to convey unshakable trust in Him because of who He is and the profound impact of His death, burial, and resurrection. Therefore, this trust eliminates my apprehension about His ability to provide for me in all areas of my life, so I am confidently abiding in Him. This context provides valuable lessons for someone who is interested in a serious relationship with Christ. The above text outlines three things that will make our relationship fruitful and productive:

1. It presents Jesus as the only true vine.
2. It emphasizes our responsibility for a fruitful relationship.
3. It also warns us of the danger of neglecting the commandments.

Jesus uses the imagery of the vine and its branches to describe His union with the believers, and He makes the point that without interconnectedness, total reliance, and dependence for sustenance, the believer will die. He explains to His disciples that fruit-bearing is not instantaneous; it is the result of a process of discipline, which involves spending time in prayer, studying the scriptures, and seeking a deep spiritual connection with Him. The same process applies to believers today; just as it is incumbent on the branch to remain connected, in this same light, the believer is encouraged to remain connected to Jesus in a rich relationship since that is the only way he or she can be effective, fruitful, and productive.

THE TRUE VINE

Jesus is the True Vine. Jesus serves as the foundation that grounds believers in their faith. He provides them with vital sustenance for their spiritual growth and empowers them to become fruitful followers (see Colossians 2:6-7). It is worth noting that while the vine does not directly bear fruit, it empowers the branches to produce fruit, highlighting the essential connection believers have with Him, without which fruitfulness would not be possible. Therefore, the believer must be fully dependent on Him in order to remain alive.

In the same way branches depend on the vine for nourishment, Christians should rely on Jesus for their spiritual strength, guidance, and sustenance. We must acknowledge our need for Him in every aspect of life. Jesus said, *"I am the true vine; abide in me."* The phrase "abide in Me, and the branch cannot bear fruit on its own" conveys a profound spiritual truth that underscores the exclusive role of Christ as the sole source of fruitfulness and productivity in the life of a believer. This theological principle illuminates the unique and irreplaceable relationship between Christ and His followers, emphasizing that all efforts to produce spiritual fruit are in vain apart from this connection.

The metaphor of the vine and branches illustrates that believers derive their spiritual vitality and nourishment from their union with Christ. This theological concept emphasizes several crucial points:

1. **Dependency on Christ:** Believers are utterly reliant on Christ for their spiritual life, growth, and the production of fruit. Any attempt to bear fruit apart from this connection is futile.

2. **Fruit as evidence:** Fruit-bearing serves as evidence of a genuine, thriving relationship with Christ. It represents the transformation and spiritual growth that occurs when believers abide in Him. Without this connection, there can be no authentic Christian living or fruitfulness.

3. **Mutual cooperation:** Just as branches cooperate with the vine to bear fruit, believers collaborate with Christ in their spiritual journey. Christ provides the divine enablement and resources; believers must actively respond in faith and obedience. He is the life-giving source of the believer. Therefore, the

believer must be fully dependent on Him in order to remain alive.

The believer will bear spiritual fruit as long as he remains connected to the vine. Galatians 5:22-23 gives an outline of the fruit of the Spirit. The concept of the "fruit of the Spirit" refers to a singular fruit with nine distinct segments or characteristics. These qualities are not separate fruits but rather interconnected aspects of a believer's character that are cultivated and displayed through a close relationship with God. There are also nine gifts of the Spirit that are given to the believers by the Holy Spirit, and these should not be confused with the fruit of the Spirit. The gifts are given, but the fruit must be cultivated or developed by the believer as he/she yields him/herself to the power of the Holy Spirit, who is working in our lives to transform us into the image of Christ.

God's primary intention is never to bring destruction upon His people. However, when we deviate from His divine path and wander out of alignment with His will, He employs various means to correct us and guide us back onto the right course. This demonstrates God's love and commitment to our spiritual growth and well-being. God's ultimate intention for His people is to bless them, offer guidance, and provide them with abundant life. His desire is for us to experience His love, grace, and the fullness of our potential as His children. When we veer off course through disobedience or straying from His principles, God's response is not one of punitive destruction but rather loving correction. His actions aim to steer us away from harm and lead us back to His intended path for our lives.

God employs various means to correct us, such as conviction through His Spirit, guidance through His Word, and sometimes allowing the natural consequences of our actions to unfold. These actions are always motivated by His desire to restore our relationship with Him. God's correction ultimately aims to bring us back into alignment with His will. It is a process of refinement and transformation designed to help us become more like Christ and experience the abundant life He offers.

In the case of the branch that becomes unfruitful, the vinedresser *"takes away"* (see John 15:2). The root word for "takes away" in Greek means to raise, to lift from the ground, and/or to take up or away. God will take the unfruitful branch, lift it from the dirt of this world into which it has fallen, and give it a chance to be productive (fruitful). If a believer gets to a place where he/she is unfruitful (barren), God will use chastisement in that believer's life to help that one become fruitful again for His glory. His chastisement is always proof of His love and of our relationship with Him (see Hebrews 12:6-8).[1]

---

[1] https://www.fbcaltoona.org/site/handlers/filedownload.ashx?moduleinstan ceid=413&dataid=5163&FileName=I%20AM%20the%20True%20Vine.p df. Time 15th of Sept.2023

SUMMARY

It is essential to understand that God's intention is never to destroy His people but to lovingly correct and guide them when they go astray. His actions are rooted in a desire for our spiritual growth, alignment with His will, and a deeper relationship with Him. It becomes abundantly clear that our ability to confidently abide in Christ hinges upon our deep and intimate knowledge of Him. Through this intimate knowledge, we can securely and steadfastly remain in Him, reflecting His grace and truth in our daily lives.

DISCUSSION QUESTIONS

How does the metaphor of Jesus as the True Vine and believers as the branches shape our understanding of the Christian faith? What implications does it have for our relationship with Christ and our role as His followers?

In what ways can we actively "abide in Christ" in our daily lives to ensure we are bearing spiritual fruit? What practices or habits help us maintain a strong connection to Him as the Vine?

How can the concept of believers as branches interconnected to the True Vine inform our approach to Christian community and accountability? How does our connection to Christ impact our relationships with other believers, and how can we support one another in bearing fruit?

PRAYER

Heavenly Father,

As I meditate on the beautiful metaphor of the vine and the branches, I am struck by the profound truth it reveals about my relationship with You. You are the true Vine, the source of all life, nourishment, and sustenance, and I am but a branch, utterly dependent on You for growth, strength, and fruitfulness. This imagery humbles me and reminds me of my need to remain deeply connected to You, for apart from You, I can do nothing (see John 15:5).

Lord, I ask for Your help in developing a posture of complete dependence on You. Teach me to abide in You as a branch abides in the vine, drawing my life, identity, and purpose from You alone. Help me to recognize that every breath I take, every thought I have, and every step I make is sustained by Your grace. May I never drift from this truth or attempt to rely on my own strength, for I know that without You, I am powerless and fruitless.

Father, cultivate in me a heart that is deeply rooted in You. Just as a branch thrives when it remains connected to the vine, I long to thrive in my relationship with You. Help me to prioritize time in Your presence, to seek You in prayer, and to immerse myself in Your Word. Let these practices not be mere routines but lifelines that keep me intimately connected to You.

I also ask for the humility to surrender my will to Yours. Just as a branch does not struggle against the vine but simply receives what it needs, help me to trust in Your provision and guidance. Teach me to yield to Your pruning, even when it is painful, knowing that it is for my growth and for Your glory. May I embrace every season of life—whether times of abundance or times of refining—with faith and gratitude, trusting that You are always working for my good. Lord, I pray that my life will bear fruit that glorifies You. May the evidence of my connection to You be seen in my love, joy, peace, patience, kindness, goodness, faithfulness, gentleness, and self-control (see Galatians 5:22-23). Let my life be a testament to Your faithfulness and a reflection of Your character.

Thank You for the gift of this relationship, for the privilege of being grafted into Your life-giving vine. Help me live each day with awareness of this connection, and may my life bring honour to Your name.

Amen.

CHAPTER 6

RELATIONSHIP WITH THE HOLY SPIRIT

The Holy Spirit was sent by God in response to Jesus' prayer for His disciples.

"I have manifested Your name to the men whom You have given Me out of the world. They were Yours, You gave them to Me, and they have kept Your word. Now they have known that all things which You have given Me are from You. For I have given to them the words which You have given Me, and they have received them, and have known surely that I came forth from You; and they have believed that You sent Me." (John 17:6 - AMPC).

While Jesus was with the disciples, He did all the work in terms of healing the sick, feeding the multitudes, and raising the dead, among other things. But now that He had finished His earthly ministry, the disciples would have to continue living and operating in a very hostile world and needed divine power and presence. So, in addition to praying for them, Jesus instructed them to separate themselves from the familiar and go to the secret place, which for them was an upper room in Jerusalem. There, they were instructed to "wait" until they were endowed with power.

"And, behold, I send the promise of my Father upon you: but tarry ye in the city of Jerusalem, until ye be endued with power from on high. And He led them out as far as to Bethany, and He lifted up His hands, and blessed them. And it came to pass, while He blessed them, He was parted from them, and carried up into heaven." (Luke 24:49-51 – KJV).

THE HOLY GHOST POWER

"And when the day of Pentecost was fully come, they were all with one accord in one place. And suddenly there came a sound from heaven as of a rushing mighty wind, and it filled all the house where they were sitting. And there appeared unto them cloven tongues like as of fire, and it sat upon each of them." (Acts 2:1-3 – KJV).

The disciples received the authentic raw power of God, which was needed to minister to the world. Conversely, as the people of God, we need the same enduement; therefore, we must dwell in the secret place with God.

Those who are led by the Spirit are the sons of God; the Holy Spirit comes to lead and guide us into all truth.

"Oh Lord I know the way of man is not in himself; it is not in man that walks to direct his own steps." (Jeremiah 10:23 - NKJV).

That is why the Holy Spirit comes alongside us to guide us and give us direction as we face the vicissitudes of life, as the disciples of Jesus and the early church were not left alone to deal with opposition and persecution. We, as His followers, enjoy the same rights and privileges, so do not forsake the secret place.

"And I will pray the Father, and he shall give you another Comforter, that he may abide with you for ever; Even the Spirit of truth; whom the world cannot receive, because it seeth him not, neither knoweth him: but ye know him; for the dwelleth with you, and shall be in you. I will not leave you comfortless: I will come to you." (John 14:16-17 - KJV).

Surrendering one's desires, fears, and control to the leading of the Holy Spirit is vital in accessing the secret place. When individuals yield to the work of the Holy Spirit within them, they can be guided into deeper spiritual experiences; these experiences will cause them to encounter the secret place in a transformative way. The precious gift of the Holy Spirit has been bestowed upon us by our gracious heavenly Father. The Holy Spirit is given to us with a profound purpose—to unveil and reveal Jesus Christ to our hearts and minds.

"When the Spirit of truth comes, He will guide you into all the truth, for He will not speak on His own authority, but

whatever He hears He will speak, and He will declare to you the things that are to come." (John 16:13 – ESV).

In our pursuit of knowing and experiencing Jesus, we are not left to our own limited understanding. God, in His infinite wisdom and love, has provided the Holy Spirit as our guide and teacher. Through the work of the Spirit, the veil is lifted, and the depths of Jesus' character, teachings, and redemptive work are unveiled before us. We hear the Psalmist's lament, *"Make me to go in the path of thy understanding." (Psalm 119:33-37 - KJV).*

The Holy Spirit takes the words and truths of scripture, breathes life into them, and allows them to penetrate the depths of our souls. Through the Holy Spirit's ministry, we can perceive and comprehend the embodiment of Jesus— His deity, sacrificial love, teachings, compassion, and role as Saviour and Lord.

In the depths of our hearts, the Holy Spirit testifies to the reality of Jesus' presence and work. He brings conviction of sin, leading us to repentance and faith in Jesus. He empowers us with spiritual gifts, equipping us to live as Christ's ambassadors in the world. The Holy Spirit enables us to experience the transformative power of Jesus' love as we conform to His image and are empowered to walk in obedience to His teachings.

As we yield to the work of the Holy Spirit, our hearts are opened to encounter Jesus in a deeply personal and intimate way. He becomes more than a historical figure or a distant concept—He becomes our living and present reality. The Holy Spirit invites us into a dynamic and ongoing relationship with Jesus, where His grace and truth are continually transforming us.

Let us embrace the gift of the Holy Spirit with gratitude and surrender. May we invite His presence into our lives and allow Him to reveal the fullness of Jesus to us. May our hearts be continually awakened and enlightened by the Holy Spirit so that we may know Jesus more deeply, love Him more fervently, and reflect His life-giving presence to the world around us.

SUMMARY

The Holy Spirit, sent by God in response to Jesus' prayer, serves as a perpetual Comforter and Spirit of truth for believers. Unlike the world, which cannot perceive or know Him, believers recognize His presence within them. The Holy Spirit affirms Jesus' reality, convicts of sin, guides to repentance and faith, and empowers with spiritual gifts for living as Christ's representatives. Through the Spirit, believers experience Jesus' transformative love, becoming more like Him and obeying His teachings. By yielding to the Spirit, believers deepen their personal relationship with Jesus, moving beyond historical or abstract understanding to encounter Him as a living, present reality, continually shaped by His grace and truth.

DISCUSSION QUESTIONS

In John 14:16-17, Jesus promises the Holy Spirit as the Helper who will be with us forever. How does the presence of the Holy Spirit in our lives contribute to our ability to dwell in the secret place with God? How can believers actively engage in fellowship with the Holy Spirit to experience His guidance and empowerment in their daily walk with God?

Romans 8:14 states, *"For all who are led by the Spirit of God are sons of God" (KJV)*. What does it mean to be led by the Holy Spirit, and how does this lead to a deeper connection with God in the secret place? How can surrendering to the Holy Spirit's leading impact our decision-making and spiritual growth?

Galatians 5:22-23 lists the fruit of the Spirit, which includes love, joy, peace, patience, kindness, goodness, faithfulness, gentleness, and self-control. How does cultivating these qualities through fellowship with the Holy Spirit enable believers to create a more conducive environment for dwelling in the secret place with God? How can a surrendered life to the Holy Spirit manifest these fruits in one's relationship with God and others?

PRAYER

Dear Heavenly Father,

We come before You with hearts full of gratitude for the incredible gift of the Holy Spirit; Your presence dwelling within us. Thank You for sending Him to be our Comforter, Guide, and Teacher, leading us into all truth and revealing the heart of Jesus to us. We are in awe of how the Holy Spirit empowers us, convicts us of sin, and transforms us into the image of Christ.

Father, we acknowledge our need for complete surrender. Please help us to yield every area of our hearts, minds, and wills to the Holy Spirit's work. Father, where we are resisting your Holy Spirit, please give us humility; where we are stubborn, soften our hearts; and where we are weak, strengthen us by Your power. Teach us to walk in step with You daily, trusting Your directive and guidance even when the path is unclear.

May the Holy Spirit deepen our relationship with You, drawing us into greater intimacy with Jesus. Let His truth illuminate our minds, His love fills our hearts, and His power flows through our lives as we serve and continue to be Your witnesses in the world. Please help us to surrender our plans, desires, and fears, asking that Your will be done in and through us.

Amen.

CHAPTER 7

THE HEART OF AN INTERCESSOR

Jesus established precedence for prayer. He prayed before dawn; He prayed all night before choosing the disciples. This prayer culture was modelled by the early church. They met in houses to pray. They prayed in the temple concerning ministerial matters and how to do humanitarian acts of kindness, taking care of widows and orphans, the marginalized and defenseless among them. James 1:27 posits, *"Religion that is pure and undefiled before God the Father is this: to visit orphans and widows in their affliction, and to keep oneself unstained from the world." (KJV).*

Acts of ministry must be executed from time spent in the secret place with the Father. So, praying in the secret place should become a ministry model for us today.

We are living in a very hostile postmodern society; evidently, we will not be effective witnesses unless we do as Jesus and His disciples did. We must begin to pray like the disciples in Acts. *"And now, Lord, behold their threatening:*

and grant unto thy servants, that with all boldness they may speak thy word, by stretching forth thine hand to heal; and that signs and wonders may be done by the name of thy holy child Jesus." (Acts 4:29-30 - KJV).

So, as we prepare ourselves in prayer, the Lord will confirm His Word among us as He did for the disciples.

"And they went forth, and preached everywhere, the Lord working with them, and confirming the word with signs following." (Mark 16:20 – KJV).

CLOSE THE DOOR

A closed door depicts privacy, confidence, trust, and intimacy. We maintain close communication with whoever our audience may be, so we need to approach prayer accordingly. God is a relational God and He loves to communicate with His sons and daughters. Hence, prayer should be done relationally. It is a time to reverence and hallow the name of God.

The place of prayer is a place of revelation and impartation; it should not be used only for petition and supplication. Although these are very important elements in prayer, if we confine ourselves to this realm, we will not enjoy the richness of prayer, which is really a conversation with Abba, so we should pray in secret to be rewarded openly.

In Matthew 6:6-8, Jesus invited us to a relational and conversational experience, hence shutting the door. He said, *"But thou, when thou prayest, enter thy closet, and when thou hast shut thy door, pray to thy Father which is in secret; and thy Father which seeth in secret shall reward thee openly. But when ye pray, use not vain repetitions, as the heathen do: for they think that they shall be heard for their much speaking. Be not ye, therefore, like unto them: for your father knoweth what things ye have need of, before ye ask him." (KJV).*

The closet or secret place is where spiritual transactions take place, lives are transformed, and destinies are shaped. Let us consider two individuals whose lives were changed because of an encounter with God in the secret place. Jacob's life was completely transformed as he lay before God in secret prayer on his way back home to meet with his brother, whom he had wronged many years ago. Prior to the encounter, Jacob sent a series of presents to Esau as a way to make him happy before they see each other. But before meeting Esau, Jacob decided to rest for the night in a camping spot. Unexpectedly, a man appears and starts wrestling with him. As the struggle continued, it became clear that this man was God Himself. Jacob received a name change and a destiny-defining moment (see Genesis 32:24). Jacob was no longer a conniving, deceptive, and deceitful person who disregarded the morals and values in God's Word and intentionally deceived his father in his old years. The Bible recalls the old man as trembling violently and uncontrollably when he realised he was deceived by his son Jacob (see

Genesis 27:33). However, subsequent to his encounter with the angel, Jacob became one of the Patriarchs and father of the twelve tribes of Israel.

Let me mention Moses, the Servant of the Lord, briefly, as I will be referencing him in another chapter. After his divine selection by God to lead the children of Israel to the promised land, he embarked on a remarkable journey of transformation, from initially struggling with a stutter to ultimately becoming the instrument of God's voice. He underwent profound changes, overcoming his anger and frustration; he tragically committed murder but later emerged as the meekest individual on the face of the earth. Throughout this transitional journey, a pivotal aspect was the time he spent alone with God.

These solitary moments held great significance in shaping his character and mission. In those moments of profound and intimate interactions with God face-to-face, Moses gleaned the essence of divine intercession. He discovered the Father's heart, which epitomized love, compassion, and mercy, withholding judgment and always extending compassion to those in dire need of it.

"And the Lord said unto Moses, Go, get thee down; for thy people, which thou broughtest out of the land of Egypt, have corrupted themselves: They have turned aside quickly out of the way which I commanded them: they have made them a molten calf, and have worshipped it, and have sacrificed thereunto, and said, These be thy gods, O Israel, which have

brought thee up out of the land of Egypt. And the Lord said unto Moses, I have seen this people, and, behold, it is a stiffnecked people: Now therefore let me alone, that my wrath may wax hot against them, and that I may consume them: and I will make of thee a great nation. And Moses besought the Lord his God, and said, Lord, why doth thy wrath wax hot against thy people, which thou hast brought forth out of the land of Egypt with great power, and with a mighty hand? Wherefore should the Egyptians speak, and say, For mischief did he bring them out, to slay them in the mountains, and to consume them from the face of the earth? Turn from thy fierce wrath, and repent of this evil against thy people. Remember Abraham, Isaac, and Israel, thy servants, to whom thou swarest by thine own self, and saidst unto them, I will multiply your seed as the stars of heaven, and all this land that I have spoken of will I give unto your seed, and they shall inherit it for ever. And the Lord repented of the evil which he thought to do unto his people." (Exodus 32:7-14 – KJV).

Moses' intercession marks the pivotal moment when God reaffirms His commitment to remain present with His people throughout their journey in the wilderness. It also marks a significant attribute of Moses; he was more interested in protecting the name of God and not making a name for himself. He was selfless, compassionate, and merciful, which are important attributes for an intercessor.

SUMMARY

The place of prayer is a place of revelation and impartation; it should not be used only for petition and supplication. Although these are very important elements in prayer, if we confine ourselves to this realm, we will not enjoy the richness of prayer, which is really a conversation with Abba. Sometimes, without making any formal request, we leave with many blessings just by spending time with Him. My encouragement to us is that we make our prayer time more relational and not so much request-oriented. In another chapter, I will say more about "Shutting the Door," a principle I have learned to be very effective.

DISCUSSION QUESTIONS

In Matthew 6:6, Jesus encourages believers to pray in secret, and their Father, who sees in secret, will reward them openly. How does the act of private prayer contribute to dwelling in the secret place with God? What are some practical strategies for maintaining a consistent and meaningful prayer life that strengthens one's connection with God?

Apostle Paul instructs in 1 Thessalonians 5:17 to *"pray without ceasing" (KJV)*. How can the practice of continuous prayer align with the concept of dwelling in the secret place? How does an ongoing conversation with God throughout the day impact one's relationship with Him and one's ability to experience His presence in daily life?

Psalm 34:17 says, *"The righteous cry out, and the Lord hears them; He delivers them from all their troubles."* (*NIV*). How does prayer serve as a means of seeking refuge and connection with God in times of trouble and adversity, ultimately contributing to dwelling in the secret place of His presence? What role do trust and dependence on God play in the effectiveness of prayer in this context?

PRAYER

Abba Father,

I come before You, not with a list, but with a longing to know You more deeply, to sit in Your presence, to hear Your heart and feel the rhythm of Your Spirit. Thank You for the gift of prayer — not just as a place of asking, but as a sacred space of revelation and impartation. Here, in this quiet place, You speak what words cannot capture. You pour into me truth, identity, wisdom, and peace. You pour into me Yourself and leave me in awe.

Father, please forgive me for the times I've reduced prayer to a transaction when You have always intended it to be communion. Teach me to rest in Your presence, listen more than I speak, and receive without always requesting.

Let my heart be still before You, and my soul awakened by Your whispers, promptings, and stillness. Even when I ask for nothing, may I leave with everything—grace upon grace, just because I've been with You. Thank You that You delight in the time we share. Shape my prayer life to be more relational, honest, and reflective of Your deep, abiding love for me.

I long to shut the door and meet You in the secret place. May that place become my dwelling, not my occasional visit, so that from that place, my life will overflow with Your presence.

In Jesus' name.
Amen.

CHAPTER 8

APPROPRIATING AND AFFIRMING THE WORD

"Death and life are in the power of the tongue: and they that love it shall eat the fruit thereof." (Proverbs 18:21 - KJV).

It is important that we say what the Word says and not what the prognosis says. This does not mean you will deny the happenings or the current situation, but you must not let it overshadow your confession.

You and I must agree with the Word of God. Do not leave the responsibility to others to speak over your life; you must speak over your life. Listen to how the Psalmist speaks in these verses. The Psalmist declares, *"I will say of the Lord He is my refuge, and my fortress, my God in him will I trust." (Psalm 91:2 - KJV).*

Children of God need to openly declare that they trust in God regardless of the circumstances. I affirm that God is my go-to person; I affirm that I am abiding in Him and He in me, so I feel a sense of being sheltered. God as my stronghold gives the idea of a military camp with soldiers, so even if danger is lurking, I am securely kept in my fortress. Hallelujah! How about you, my friend? What are you saying about the Lord? What is your confession?

In ancient times, a stronghold was a fortress or a walled city where people sought shelter from their enemies. By describing the Lord as the "stronghold of my life," the Psalmist emphasizes the impenetrable nature of God's protection. Where are you on your journey? Are you sick? Or are you in a cave like David, hiding from Saul, who is seeking his life? Are you in a pit like Joseph being sold by his brothers? Are you confused? Feeling hopeless and helpless? Pull yourself together and appropriate the truth of God's Word; speak over yourself.

We must confidently declare the end result and not the existing problem; the Psalmist said, *"Surely He shall deliver me from the snare of the fowler and from the noisome pestilence."* (*Psalm 91:3 - KJV*). The Psalmist spoke emphatically and confidently, *"God shall cover me with His feathers and under His wings I will take refuge. His truth shall be my shield and buckler. No evil shall befall me and no plague will come nigh my dwelling."* (Psalm. 91:4 - KJV).

"No weapon that is formed against thee shall prosper; and every tongue that shall rise against thee in judgment thou shalt condemn. This is the heritage of the servants of the

Lord, and their righteousness is of me, saith the Lord." (Isaiah 54:17 – KJV).

Declare what the Word says and not what the situation or circumstance dictates. Truth is irrevocable, but facts change based on circumstances. The Psalmist declares, *"I will say of the Lord He is my refuge and my fortress; my God in Him will I trust. Surely, he shall deliver thee from the snare of the fowler and from the noisome pestilence, he shall cover thee with his feathers and under his wings shalt thou trust. His shield shall be thy shield and buckler." (Psalm. 91:2 - KJV).*

Hallelujah! Praise God.

Agreeing with the Word of God by speaking it builds our faith and confidence in God. Similarly, confessing the existing negative situation diminishes our faith.

"The spirit of a man will sustain his infirmity." *(Proverbs 18:14a - KJV).*

So, where are you on your journey? What is it that you are grappling with? If you are facing sickness and disease, begin to declare the Word of God over your life. Use the scriptures that speak to your immediate situation and wait for the Holy Spirit to quicken it in your heart. Do not panic or give into fear. Fear is a spirit; it comes from the evil one (see 2 Timothy 1:7).

Speaking what the Word said instead of what the problem is will encourage faith and diminish doubts. Romans 10:17 states that faith comes by hearing the Word of God. So, since faith comes by hearing, I submit to you that doubt comes by hearing as well. As a result, we need to pay keen attention to what we are repeatedly hearing. Faith is released through action, and one very important action is confessing the Word of God repeatedly. So let us continue to affirm that God is my hiding place, refuge, and fortress, despite the circumstances. I must confidently declare who God is to me even though I might be experiencing the opposite of what I am saying. God promised that He would never leave me or forsake me. *"Death and life are in the power of the tongue, and those who love it will eat the fruit thereof." (Proverbs 18:21 - KJV).* So then, we must decide what kind of fruit we want by speaking or planting the correct seed to reap the harvest that we are expecting. It is insanity to do the wrong thing and expect to get the right result.

"A good man out of the good treasure of his heart bringeth forth that which is good; and an evil man out of the evil treasure of his heart bringeth forth that which is evil: for of the abundance of the heart his mouth speaketh." (Luke 6:45 - KJV).

"Let us hold fast the profession of our faith without wavering; (for he is faithful that promised;)" (Hebrews 10:23 – KJV).

SUMMARY

The power of our words is profound, as *"death and life are in the tongue"* (see Proverbs 18:21). It is crucial to speak God's Word over our lives rather than focusing on negative circumstances or diagnoses.

While we acknowledge reality, we must not let it overshadow our confession of faith. Therefore, we build faith and confidence in Him by declaring God's promises, like the Psalmist who affirmed God as his refuge, fortress, and protector.

Speaking God's truth over our lives—whether in sickness, fear, or despair—shifts our focus from problems to His promises. Faith grows by hearing and declaring God's Word while confessing negativity weakens it. So, no matter the challenge, we must boldly affirm scripture, trusting in God's protection and deliverance, for His truth is unchanging, even when circumstances shift.

DISCUSSION QUESTIONS

Proverbs 18:21 states, *"Death and life are in the power of the tongue." (KJV).* How does aligning our words with the Word of God impact our lives and circumstances? What Biblical examples can you find where individuals' declarations or confessions of faith played a significant role in their experiences?

Hebrews 4:12 describes the Word of God as *"living and active, sharper than any two-edged sword"* (*NIV*). How does regularly meditating on and speaking God's Word align our hearts and words with His truth? How can this practice help us manifest the fruit of our lips in the form of blessings, encouragement, and faith-filled declarations in our daily lives?

In Psalm 19:14, David prays, *"Let the words of my mouth, and the meditation of my heart, be acceptable in thy sight, O Lord, my strength, and my redeemer." (KJV)*. How can we ensure that our words align with God's Word, and what are the benefits of doing so in our relationship with God and others? How can a commitment to speaking in agreement with the Word of God enhance our spiritual growth and impact the lives of those around us?

PRAYER

Heavenly Father,
We come before You with hearts full of gratitude for the power You have placed within our words. Your Word reminds us that *"death and life are in the power of the tongue, and those who love it will eat its fruit." (Proverbs 18:21 – KJV)*. Lord, we recognize the immense responsibility and privilege we have to speak life, truth, and faith into every situation we face. Help us to align our words with Your Word, declaring what You say over our lives rather than what circumstances or the world may dictate.

Father, we understand that this does not mean ignoring or denying the reality of our challenges, but it means refusing to let those challenges overshadow our confession of faith. We choose to agree with Your promises, knowing that Your Word is truth and life. We take responsibility for speaking Your Word over our lives rather than relying solely on others to do so. As we declare Your promises, our faith strengthens, and our confidence in You grows.

Lord, please guard our hearts and tongues from speaking words of doubt, fear, or negativity, for we know that such confessions can weaken our faith and hinder Your work in our lives. So, we ask instead to let our words reflect the truth of Your Word, bringing life, hope, and encouragement.

As Proverbs 18:14a says, *"the spirit of a man will sustain his infirmity,"* therefore, we trust that as we speak in agreement with Your Spirit, we will be sustained and strengthened in every trial. Teach us to be intentional with our words, using them to build up, encourage, and declare Your promises. May our tongues be instruments of life, bringing glory to Your name and advancing Your kingdom. Thank You, Father, for the power of Your Word and the authority You have given us to speak life into every situation. In Jesus' name, we pray.

Amen.

CHAPTER 9

WALKING WITH GOD (PART ONE)

The Bible introduces us to several remarkable individuals who walked closely with God throughout their lifetimes. Let us focus on the lives of two exemplary servants, exploring their unique journeys of faith and the valuable lessons they offer to believers today. But first, let us examine what it means to walk with God.

"Walking with God" implies a steadfast and unwavering commitment to maintaining a close relationship with Him. It signifies that regardless of the challenges and obstacles we encounter along our journey of faith, we remain resolute and determined, never retreating from our faith and trust in God. This concept of "walking with God" embodies several important aspects:

1. **Consistency:** Walking with God suggests a continuous and unbroken connection with Him. It is not an intermittent or occasional engagement with faith but a daily, habitual practice. It means

consistently seeking God's presence and guidance in our lives, not just when convenient. I am reminded of a hymn that states, *"Hand in hand we walk each day. Hand in hand along the way. Walking thus I cannot stray. Hand in hand with Jesus."*

2. **Persistence:** Persistency means continuing firmly or obstinately in an opinion or course of action despite difficulty or opposition. So then, in the face of challenges, setbacks, and trials, a person who is walking with God should remain persistent in their faith. They should not give up or abandon their trust in Him even though they are experiencing all sorts of challenges, whether sickness, financial setbacks, family, or just interpersonal relationships. Instead, they should draw strength from their relationship with God to persevere through difficulties.

3. **Trust and Dependency.** This idea of trust cannot be overemphasised because walking with God requires deep trust and dependency on Him. It means relying on His wisdom, strength, and guidance to navigate life's challenges. Even when circumstances seem daunting, those who walk with God trust that He will lead them on the right path. Psalm 23:1- 4 says, *"The Lord is my shepherd; I shall not want. He maketh me to lie down in green pastures: he leadeth me beside the still waters. He restoreth my soul: He leadeth me in the paths of righteousness for His name's sake. Yea, though I walk through the valley of the shadow*

of death, I will fear no evil: for thou art with me; thy rod and thy staff they comfort me." (KJV). Believers find true success in their Christian journey by cultivating profound trust and dependency on God. This truth, evident in Proverbs 3:5-6, emphasizes surrendering totally to the guidance and leading of the Holy Spirit, which is not a sign of weakness but a source of strength. This dynamic partnership will ultimately transform our walk and deepen our commitment to God.

4. **Spiritual Growth:** A consistent and persistent walk with God will result in spiritual growth and maturity. It is through the trials and challenges that our faith is refined and strengthened. *"Beloved, think it not strange concerning the fiery trial which is to try you, as though some strange thing happened unto you; But rejoice, in as much as ye are partakers of Christ's sufferings; that, when his glory shall be revealed, ye may be glad also with exceeding joy" (1 Peter 4:12-13 - KJV).* Those who walk with God understand that difficulties are opportunities for growth. When individuals consistently and persistently walk with God, they become examples to others. Their unwavering faith can inspire and encourage those around them to also trust in God and remain steadfast in their faith journeys.

Let's look at Enoch, the son of Jared, a descendant of Enosh, who was a son of Seth. Seth was the third son that God gave to Adam and Eve after the death of Abel (see Genesis 4:25; Genesis 5:18-25). However, the Bible does not go into detail about this account. We only know that after the birth of his eldest son, Methuselah, Enoch walked with God for three hundred years, and then he was taken up. *"And Enoch walked with God: and he was not; for God took him" (Genesis 5:24 – KJV).*

Have you ever wondered what the relationship between Enoch and God looked like? Well, I have, and I get lost in my imagination. I remember one of those moments from my past when, as an only child, I would find myself outdoors, engrossed in play with my imaginary friends. The time spent with them was so joyful and peaceful that I often preferred staying outside, reluctant to return to the company of my family. I know this does not depict the true imagery of their relationship, but it is at least a cause for reflection. Enoch's profound relationship with God evokes deep reflections. His intimacy and obedience to God's principles set a remarkable example. It transcends a conventional understanding of death for the believer. Death is just a transport that takes us home to be with our Lord and Saviour. God was so impressed by Enoch's commitment that He chose to bring him home with Him, and the same will happen to us as we continue to walk with Him. Enoch's obedience goes beyond mere ritual; it is a heartfelt dedication, a deliberate obedience to God, and his example urges us to foster a genuine relationship with God.

Let us take a closer look at the relationship between Abraham and God. Abraham originally came from a pagan country where idol worship was the norm, and it is unclear if he had any previous experience with God. Yet, when God called him, he unquestioningly followed. Abraham embarked on this journey based on his faith, trusting that he would eventually reach the destination God had promised him.

"Now the Lord had said unto Abram, Get thee out of thy country, and from thy kindred, and from thy father's house, unto a land that I will shew thee, and I will make of thee a great nation, and I will bless thee, and make thy name great; and thou shalt be a blessing, and I will bless them that bless thee, and curse him that curseth thee: and in thee shall all families of the earth be blessed. So, Abram departed, as the Lord had spoken unto him; and Lot went with him: and Abram was seventy and five years old when he departed out of Haran." (Genesis 12:1-4 - KJV).

"By faith Abraham, when he was called to go out into a place which he should after receive for an inheritance, obeyed; and he went out, not knowing whither he went. By faith he sojourned in the land of promise, as in a strange country, dwelling in tabernacles with Isaac and Jacob, the heirs with him of the same promise: For he looked for a city which hath foundations, whose builder and maker is God." (Hebrews 11:8-10 - KJV).

The same is true for all of us. We must abandon ourselves to God and allow Him to take us where He wants to take us. Life is a journey with a tour guide called experience. We move from one destination or encounter to another with confidence that the next encounter will be better than the last. The patriarchs of old, especially those mentioned in Hebrews 11, all died in faith, confidence, and trust in God, even though they did not receive the promise that they expected in their lifetime.

"And these all, having obtained a good report through faith, received not the promise: God having provided some better thing for us, that they without us should not be made perfect." (Hebrews 11:39-40 - KJV).

"Walking with God" means having a continuous relationship with Him, even through difficult times. It requires steadfast trust, persistence, and a commitment to spiritual growth. Those who walk with God benefit personally and serve as examples of faith for others to follow. Though these individuals lived in different times and faced unique challenges, their stories are relevant to believers of all generations. Their steadfast devotion to God provides a timeless blueprint for nurturing and sustaining a vibrant walk with Him. By exploring the journeys of these remarkable servants, we can find inspiration and encouragement for our own spiritual walks. Their stories illuminate the possibilities of a deep and fulfilling relationship with God and inspire us to seek a closer connection with Him in our own lives.

The lives of these biblical servants are not just historical narratives but living testimonies that continue to resonate with contemporary believers. Their faith journeys offer valuable lessons on trust, perseverance, obedience, and the transformative power of a close relationship with God. Their commitment to God provides a timeless blueprint for nurturing and sustaining a vibrant walk with the divine.

SUMMARY

The Bible highlights the lives of remarkable individuals who walked closely with God, offering timeless lessons for believers today. "Walking with God" signifies a steadfast commitment to maintaining a close relationship with Him, regardless of life's challenges. This concept encompasses several key aspects, for example, consistency and persistence. In the face of challenges, setbacks, and trials, a person who is walking with God should remain persistent in their faith. We should not give up or abandon our trust in Him. We should draw strength from our relationship with God to persevere through difficulties.

DISCUSSION QUESTIONS

Both Abraham and Enoch displayed exceptional faith and obedience in their walk with God. How can we apply their trust in God's promises and their willingness to follow His guidance to our own lives? What challenges do we face in maintaining such faith and obedience in today's world?

Enoch is described as having "walked with God," and Abraham is known as the "friend of God." What does their close relationship with God teach us about the importance of intimacy with God in our daily lives? How can we cultivate a deep and meaningful relationship with God amid our busy, modern lifestyles?

Abraham and Enoch set a strong example of faith for the future. How can their faith encourage us to do the same for our families and communities? What simple actions can we take to share our faith with the next generation and be good spiritual role models like they were?

PRAYER

Heavenly Father,
We come before You with hearts full of gratitude for the examples of faith and obedience demonstrated by Enoch and Abraham. Thank You for showing us what it means to walk closely with You—consistently, persistently, and with steadfast trust. Lord, we desire to cultivate the same depth of relationship with You that Enoch had marked by intimacy, obedience, and a heart fully devoted to You. Holy Father, please help us walk hand in hand with You daily, seeking Your presence and guidance at every moment.

Father, like Abraham, we acknowledge that stepping out in faith can be challenging, especially when the path ahead is unclear. Strengthen our trust in You, Lord, so we may rely on Your wisdom and strength rather than our own. Teach us to depend on You completely, knowing You will lead us on the right path, even through valleys and trials.

Father, we ask for the grace to remain persistent in our faith, no matter what challenges we face—whether sickness, financial struggles, relational difficulties, or uncertainty. Help us to draw strength from our relationship with You and to persevere with hope and confidence in Your promises.

Father, we are praying for spiritual growth. Please refine our faith through the trials we encounter and use our lives as testimonies to inspire others to trust in You. Cause our walk with You to become a light to those around us, pointing them to Your love, faithfulness, and power.

Thank You, Lord, for the assurance that walking with You leads to life, transformation, and eternal fellowship with You. Help us walk faithfully, just as Enoch and Abraham did, so we may bring glory to Your name. In Jesus' name, we pray.

Amen.

CHAPTER 10

WALKING WITH GOD (PART TWO)

"Blessed is the man that walketh not in the counsel of the ungodly, nor standeth in the way of sinners, nor sitteth in the seat of the scornful. But his delight is in the law of the Lord; and in his law doth he meditate day and night. And he shall be like a tree planted by the rivers of water, that bringeth forth his fruit in his season; his leaf also shall not wither; and whatsoever he doeth shall prosper. The ungodly are not so: but are like the chaff which the wind driveth away. Therefore, the ungodly shall not stand in the judgment, or sinners in the congregation of the righteous. For the Lord knoweth the way of the righteous: but the way of the ungodly shall perish." (Psalm 1:1-6 – KJV).

Psalm 1 provides a clear and vivid contrast between two distinct individuals or groups of people. It paints a stark picture of two divergent paths and lifestyles, illustrating the choices and consequences awaiting those following each path. It presents a fundamental choice that every individual faces—the choice between two paths. One path leads to a life characterized by righteousness, godliness, and spiritual prosperity, while the other leads to a life marked by ungodliness, sin, and spiritual barrenness.

THE RIGHTEOUS

The Psalm describes the righteous person as one who delights in God's law and meditates on it day and night. This person is like a well-nourished tree, firmly rooted by streams of water, bearing fruit in its season. The righteous path is characterized by spiritual growth, fulfilment, and a close relationship with God which encapsulates his "walk" of right living in obedience to God's Word.

"Love not the world, neither the things that are in the world. If any man loves the world, the love of the Father is not in him. For all that is in the world, the lust of the flesh (this refers to impure desires, sinful pleasures and sensual gratification), and the lust of the eyes (coveting or lusting after things that are attractive to the eyes but forbidden by God)..." (1 John 2:15-16 – KJV – emphasis mine). Those who delight in God and His Word have a root system that draws life from God, which causes them to prosper. The walk of the righteous is very significant.

THE UNGODLY

The ungodly are unrepentant sinners, who are described as follows:

1. Chaff blown away by the wind. This refers to forces they cannot see or discern by themselves. Like chaff, there is no substance in them. They are unproductive and unfruitful. Jesus referred to them as leftover trash prepared for judgment (see Matthew 3:12). Ultimately, they will be condemned by God on the day of judgment (see Matthew 25:31-46 and Revelation 6:17).

The ungodly are portrayed as separated from God's blessings and will face ultimate judgment. The ungodly path leads to spiritual emptiness, confusion, and, ultimately, separation from God. We must contend with our own sinful attitudes and desires, which result in us making poor choices. Also, Psalm 1 reminds us that our actions, attitudes, and priorities have profound implications for our spiritual well-being and ultimate destiny. It encourages us to prioritize a close relationship with God, meditate on His Word, and make choices that align with righteousness.

SUMMARY

Psalm 1 contrasts two life paths—one characterized by righteousness and godliness, the other by ungodliness and spiritual barrenness. This contrast highlights the importance of our choices and their profound impact on our spiritual journey and ultimate destiny. It encourages us to prioritize a close relationship with God, meditate on His Word, and make choices that align with righteousness. It also serves as a warning against the allure of sinful lifestyles and the spiritual consequences they entail.

According to the Psalm, when individuals *"stand in the way of sinners,"* it suggests that they place themselves in situations where they are in close proximity to those who habitually engage in sinful activities. This can occur intentionally or inadvertently. It causes them to adopt the same attitudes, values, and rationalizations that justify sinful behaviour, making it easier for them to engage in such actions. This pattern of aligning with sinners and adopting their disposition can have negative spiritual consequences. It can lead individuals away from their faith or moral principles, resulting in a compromised spiritual and ethical outlook.

DISCUSSION QUESTIONS

What does it mean to *"delight in the law of the Lord"* in Psalm 1, and how can this principle be applied to our daily lives?

Psalm 1 presents a sharp contrast between the way of the righteous and the way of the wicked. How does this Psalm characterize these two paths, and what are the consequences of following each path?

In Psalm 1, the righteous are compared to trees planted by streams of water, while the wicked are described as chaff blown away by the wind. How does this imagery relate to the concept of stability and rootedness in one's faith?

How do the contrasting paths of the righteous and the wicked in Psalm 1 help us consider the moral and spiritual choices we make, and what insights can we gain from examining the consequences of these choices in our spiritual journey?

PRAYER

Heavenly Father,
We come before You with hearts open to Your Word and Your truth. Thank You for the wisdom and guidance found in Psalm 1, which clearly shows us the contrast between the path of righteousness and the way of the ungodly. Lord, we desire to walk in the way that leads to life, rooted in You and nourished by Your Word.

Father, please help us to prioritize our relationship with You above all else. Teach us to meditate on Your Word day and night, allowing it to shape our thoughts, actions, and decisions. May Your truth be the foundation of our lives, guiding us to make choices that honour You and reflect Your righteousness.

Heavenly Father, we recognize the dangers of standing in the way of sinners or aligning ourselves with those who habitually engage in sinful behaviour. Please help us to guard our hearts and minds from the influence of ungodly attitudes, values, and rationalizations. Keep us from compromising our faith or drifting away from Your principles.

Instead, Lord, help us to be planted firmly by the streams of living water, where we can flourish and bear fruit in every season. Daddy, help us when we face temptations or find ourselves in situations that could lead us astray. Please remind us of the spiritual consequences of walking in the way of the ungodly, and please strengthen us to resist the allure of sinful lifestyles and stand firm in our faith. Surround us with godly influences and communities that encourage us to grow closer to You.

Thank You, Lord, for the promise that those who delight in Your Word and walk in Your ways are blessed, stable, and fruitful. May our lives reflect the beauty of a life rooted in You, and may we be a light to others, pointing them to the path of righteousness.

Amen.

CHAPTER 11

WALKING IN THE SPIRIT

In the Epistle to the Galatians, Apostle Paul provides a compelling exhortation to the church, urging them to wholeheartedly embrace the redemptive work accomplished by Christ as the sole means of attaining salvation. Within the context of this biblical letter, Paul passionately emphasizes that salvation is not attainable through human effort, religious rituals, or adherence to the law. Instead, he underscores that salvation is a gift graciously bestowed by God through the sacrificial work of Jesus Christ on the cross. He calls upon believers to recognize that the crucifixion and resurrection of Christ are the cornerstones of their faith. Through His death and subsequent triumph over death, Jesus has provided a way for humanity to be reconciled with God and obtain eternal salvation. This profound theological teaching goes beyond mere religious dogma. Paul's message underscores the fundamental principle that salvation cannot be earned through human merit. It is a divine gift extended to all who place their faith in Christ, acknowledging that forgiveness of sins and the promise of eternal life come only from Him.

There are three points I would like us to explore:

1. What does it mean to walk in the Spirit?
2. The conflict between the flesh and the Spirit.
3. The guidance and freedom offered by the Spirit.

According to Webster's online dictionary, walking means moving along on foot or advancing by steps, coming or going easily or readily.

Why should we walk in the Spirit? Because it is the only way to overcome the sinful desires of our human nature and have absolute victory in all areas of our lives. We must walk in the Spirit because it is a command, not a matter of convenience. Walking in the Spirit is not a cloud-nine experience. It is not being heavenly-minded and of no earthly good; instead, it is a relatable experience. It allows you to be in touch with reality and provides a firm foundation that prevents us from falling apart when confronted with life's difficulties.

What does walking in the Spirit look like? It is a daily step-by-step journey with Jesus and the Holy Spirit; it is a walk of harmony, which means that each day, I intentionally commit to a daily life that harmonizes with the teachings of Jesus and follows the guidance of the Holy Spirit. For most of us, this is not a walk in the park, but nonetheless, it is achievable, noting carefully that the operative word is "walking" and not running.

In 1 Corinthians 9:24, the Apostle Paul talks about running a race to win a prize. This analogy is used to encourage believers to live a disciplined life that is focused on achieving their spiritual goals. Similarly, walking in the Spirit is also about living a disciplined life, but it is more focused on following the guidance of the Holy Spirit. While running a race emphasizes the importance of discipline, effort, and perseverance, walking in the Spirit emphasizes the importance of surrendering one's will to God and allowing the Holy Spirit to lead and guide us. In other words, running a race is about striving to achieve a specific goal, while walking in the Spirit is about allowing God to guide us to our ultimate destination. Both require discipline and effort but have different focuses and end goals.

There is a conflict between the flesh and the Spirit. It is essential for us to recognize and appreciate the perpetual battle that ensues between our physical desires and our inner spiritual essence. This ongoing struggle is a quest for dominance and control. It is not merely an abstract concept but a fundamental part of our existence, influencing our decisions, thoughts, and emotions and shaping our character.

"Know you not, that to whom you yield yourselves servants to obey, his servants you are whom you obey, whether it be of sin unto death, or of obedience unto righteousness." (Romans 6:16 – KJV).

This internal struggle is a profound aspect of the human experience and will continue as long as life lasts, so we need to follow the instructions of the apostle Paul in Romans 12:2, *"Don't copy the behaviour and customs of this world, but let God transform you into a new person by changing the way you think. Then you will learn to know God's will for you, which is good and pleasing and perfect." (NLT).*

Let us examine some of the fleshy desires that conflict with the Spirit.

"Now the works of the flesh are manifest, which are these; adultery, fornication, uncleanness, lasciviousness, idolatry, witchcraft, hatred, variance, emulations, wrath, strife, seditions, heresies, envying, murders, drunkenness, revellings, and such like: of the which I tell you before, as I have also told you in time past, that they which do such things shall not inherit the kingdom of God." (Galatians 5:19-21 - KJV).

Please note that these are outward manifestations or expressions of an inner struggle. It is called "works" because we have to participate and engage with it.

THE HOLY SPIRIT PROVIDES GUIDANCE AND FREEDOM TO WALK IN THE SPIRIT

Apostle Paul highlights the transformative power of the Holy Spirit in the lives of believers. He encourages Christians to resist the temptation of legalism, emphasizing that salvation and righteous living do not come through the strict observance of religious laws but by accepting the sacrificial death of Christ and the promise of the Holy Spirit and the importance of yielding to the Spirit.

"And I will pray the Father, and He shall give you another Comforter, that He may abide with you for ever; Even the Spirit of truth; whom the world cannot receive, because it seeth him not, neither knoweth him: but ye know him; for he dwelleth with you, and shall be in you. I will not leave you comfortless, I will come to you." (John 14:16-18 – KJV).

This guidance reflects a profound theological concept that transcends mere legalism. Paul underscores the idea that a genuine relationship with God involves a dynamic, personal connection with the Holy Spirit. By allowing the Spirit to guide their lives, believers can experience a radical transformation from within. This transformation is evidenced by the "fruit of the Spirit" (see Galatians 5:22-23).

Walking in the Spirit is staying in step with Jesus and the Holy Spirit. Walking in the Spirit is not a sprint, neither is it a marathon. It is living in harmony with the Spirit and embracing a life that aligns with the teachings of Jesus and the guidance of the Holy Spirit.

We should try at all times and in all situations to avoid a backward retreat, which means resisting the temptation to fall behind or regress in our spiritual journey; always maintain spiritual synchronization.

We should strive to walk in step with the Holy Spirit, ensuring that our life mirrors the strides of God's presence, not running ahead but keeping up with the momentum of the Spirit.

SUMMARY

Walking in the Spirit is a profound journey that beckons us to align our lives with the divine guidance and wisdom of the Holy Spirit. It is a path marked by the pursuit of spiritual virtues, the bearing of the fruit of the Spirit, and the surrender of our own desires to the higher purpose of God. As we walk in the Spirit, we find strength, comfort, and direction in our daily lives, transcending our human nature's limitations and connecting with God's boundless grace. This spiritual walk leads us toward a life of love, peace, and purpose, empowering us to navigate the challenges of this world with faith and a steadfast commitment to live in accordance with God's will. Ultimately, walking in the Spirit makes us discover the true essence of our faith and experience the profound peace and fulfilment that can only be found in our intimate relationship with God.

DISCUSSION QUESTIONS

Galatians 5:16 admonishes us to *"Walk in the Spirit, and you shall not fulfil the lust of the flesh."* (*KJV*). What does it mean to "walk in the Spirit," and how can we practically apply this instruction to our daily lives?

Galatians 5:16 contrasts walking in the Spirit with fulfilling the lust of the flesh. How do you understand the concept of the "lust of the flesh" in your own life, and what strategies or practices have you found helpful in resisting these temptations while striving to walk in the Spirit?

The Holy Spirit plays a significant role in the Christian faith, as emphasized in Galatians 5:16. Give examples of how you seek to cultivate a deeper relationship with the Holy Spirit in your life, and what benefits have you experienced from aligning your actions and attitudes with the guidance of the Spirit?

PRAYER

Heavenly Father,
As I come before You today, I open my heart to You for Your leading. Please teach me to walk in the Spirit—to live each day step by step with Your divine guidance and holy wisdom. Let my journey not be one of mere striving but of surrender. Please help me to yield my desires, plans, and will to Your divine will and purpose for my life.

Precious Holy Spirit, Let Your presence dwell richly within me, shaping my thoughts, actions, and character. As I walk this path, may I pursue the virtues that reflect Your heart—love, joy, peace, patience, kindness, goodness, faithfulness, gentleness, and self-control.

Please cultivate in me the fruit of the Spirit that brings glory to You. May others see not just a reflection of who I am but a revelation of who You are through me. Please guide my steps, refine my motives, and strengthen me when I falter.

Dear Lord, You are aware that this journey demands consecration. Please help me to trust you wholeheartedly, renounce the works of the flesh, and embrace your truth. In Jesus' name I pray.

Amen.

CHAPTER 12

THE FRUIT OF THE SPIRIT

T he fruit of the Spirit is a profound biblical concept that highlights a collection of virtues that are to be cultivated in the lives of believers through the influence of the Holy Spirit. These virtues can be effectively sorted into three primary groups, each of which reflects distinct facets of a person's character and behaviour. Let us examine these categories and offer a more comprehensive understanding of each one.

Inward-focused virtues comprise love, joy, and peace; these are inward virtues that are expressed by every born-again Christian regardless of their current experiences.

Love is the fundamental ingredient of the fruit of the Spirit. This love is characterized by its unconditional and selfless nature, representing a profound and genuine concern for others that transcends personal interests. Love serves as the cornerstone upon which the other virtues find their equilibrium.

Joy embodies a profound and enduring sense of contentment and happiness that remains unshaken by external circumstances. It is a wellspring of inner delight that flows from one's deep connection with God. The joy of the Lord is our strength.

Peace encompasses a twofold meaning. It involves the inner serenity and harmony experienced within oneself, stemming from faith and a close relationship with God. Additionally, it extends its capacity to promote reconciliation and harmony in one's relationships with others, fostering an atmosphere of tranquillity and unity.

Then, there are the outward-focused virtues: patience, kindness, goodness, faithfulness, gentleness, and self-control.

Patience emerges as a virtue of great significance. Patience is not merely about gritting our teeth and bearing hardships but a willingness to wait with composure and grace. In the face of life's trials and tribulations, it encourages us to remain steadfast in our faith, trusting that God's timing is perfect. This patience, rooted in our relationship with God, helps us navigate the storms of life with a calm and unshaken spirit. The prophet Isaiah states, *"Those who wait on the Lord shall renew their strength. They will mount up with wings like eagles." (Isaiah 40:31 - KJV).* The wise man, Solomon, helps us understand that life's race is not given to the swift or the strong but to the one who endures to the end (see Ecclesiastes 9:11).

Kindness is a distinct quality that radiates goodwill and compassion towards others. It is about more than just holding open doors or offering a warm smile; it is an attitude of generosity and benevolence that runs deep. Kindness prompts us to extend empathy and heartfelt concern to those we encounter, seeking their well-being with a genuine and selfless spirit. In a world often marked by indifference, practicing kindness is a way to live out the love of Christ by actively demonstrating care and understanding.

Goodness draws our attention to moral excellence and the desire to do what is right and virtuous. It encompasses a commitment to ethical principles, integrity, and living a life that reflects these values. Goodness is not just about avoiding wrongdoing; it is about actively pursuing righteousness and making ethical choices. It is an internal compass that guides our actions, encouraging us to walk in the path of honesty and virtue. In a world that often presents ethical challenges, goodness becomes a beacon, illuminating the way to a life that is pleasing to God and beneficial to others.

Faithfulness means being reliable, trustworthy, and loyal—keeping promises and staying committed to God and others, as God calls us into fellowship with Christ, the ultimate example of faithfulness (see 1 Corinthians 4:2). It requires responsibility and accountability.

Gentleness, the opposite of harshness, involves being considerate, tender, and supportive in interactions rather than dominating.

Self-control is about disciplining desires, emotions, and actions, resisting temptations, and living in alignment with one's faith and values.

SUMMARY

The "fruit of the Spirit" holds deep significance for the Christian journey, providing a blueprint for character and behaviour. It is not just a checklist but virtues that reflect God's love and grace while helping believers embody Christ's character in a broken world.

DISCUSSION QUESTIONS

How can the concept of the "fruit of the Spirit" found in Galatians 5:22-23 serve as a practical guide for Christians in their daily lives? What specific challenges have you encountered in trying to cultivate these virtues, and how did you overcome them?

The "fruit of the Spirit" places a strong emphasis on love, joy, and peace as foundational virtues. In what ways have you experienced the transformative power of these virtues in your relationship with God and your interactions with others? How do they relate to the concept of Christian joy and inner peace?

Each of the virtues in the "fruit of the Spirit" represents a distinct facet of character and conduct. How do you see the interplay between the inward virtues like patience, kindness, and goodness and the outward virtues like faithfulness, gentleness, and self-control? How can this balance be achieved in our efforts to reflect Christ's character in our lives?

PRAYER

Heavenly Father,
Thank You for the gift of Your Holy Spirit and the power of the "fruit of the Spirit" outlined in Galatians 5:22-23. We humbly ask that these virtues—love, joy, peace, patience, kindness, goodness, faithfulness, gentleness, and self-control—become the heartbeat of our daily lives. Teach us, Lord, to lean on Your Holy Spirit as our practical guide, especially when challenges arise. When impatience flares in moments of waiting, when unkind thoughts threaten to harden our hearts, or when self-control feels out of reach, remind us that Your grace is sufficient and Your strength is made perfect in our weakness.

Father, we confess the struggles we have faced in cultivating these fruits. There are days when anxiety dims our joy, resentment clouds our peace, or pride stifles our gentleness. Yet in those moments, You have been faithful to meet us. Through prayer, scripture, and the support of fellow believers, You have shown us that these virtues are not achieved by our own effort but are cultivated through surrender to Your Spirit. Help us to abide in You daily, trusting that as we remain rooted in Christ, Your fruit will grow in us naturally and abundantly.

Lord, we marvel at how love, joy, and peace have anchored our relationship with You and softened our interactions with others. Your love has taught us to forgive the unforgivable, Your joy has sustained us through sorrow, and Your peace has steadied us in chaos. These virtues are not fleeting emotions but supernatural gifts that testify to Your presence within us. We pray for a deeper experience of Christian joy—a joy unshaken by circumstances—and for Your peace to guard our hearts even in the storms of life.

As we seek to reflect Your character, show us how the inward virtues of patience, kindness, and goodness shape our private walk with You while faithfulness, gentleness, and self-control manifest outwardly in our words and actions. Teach us to balance this synergy by nurturing inner stillness through prayer so that outward gentleness flows effortlessly, cultivating private faithfulness so that public integrity becomes second nature, and practicing hidden kindness so that visible goodness shines brightly. Lord, make us vessels of Your Spirit's fruit so that others may taste and see Your goodness through us.

Amen!

CHAPTER 13

PROTECTING YOUR MENTAL HEALTH

"Wherefore gird up the loins of your mind, be sober, and hope to the end for the grace that is to be brought unto you at the revelation of Jesus Christ; As obedient children, not fashioning yourselves according to the former lusts in your ignorance: But as He which hath called you is holy, so be ye holy in all manner of conversation; Because it is written, Be ye holy." (1 Peter 1:13-16 – KJV).

What does it mean to gird up the loins of our mind? In 1 Peter 1:13, the phrase "gird up the loins of your mind" is a metaphorical expression that means preparing oneself mentally and emotionally for action or a challenge. In the ancient Near East, people wore long robes that would impede their movement, especially when running or fighting. So, they would tie their robes around their waist to free their legs and be ready for action. In the same way, Peter is encouraging his readers to mentally prepare themselves for the challenges and trials they may face as Christians.

The notion of "girding up the loins of our minds" include our capacity and readiness to face and handle life's daily challenges and demands. It signifies our mental fortitude and ability to equip ourselves with the mental and emotional resources required to navigate the complexities and adversities we encounter on a routine basis. This concept underscores the importance of mental resilience, adaptability, and the ability to confront whatever life throws at us with a prepared and determined mindset. To "gird up the loins of your mind" means to be alert and focused; it involves being disciplined in your thought life, controlling your emotions, increasing your ability to cope with stress, and being intentional about your mental and emotional state. These disciplines are important for good mental health because they help you stay grounded and focused, even in difficult situations.

In Ephesians 6:10-18, Paul encourages believers to put on the full armour of God in order to stand firm against the schemes of the devil. This includes the "belt of truth," which can be seen as a metaphorical representation of "girding up the loins." By putting on this spiritual armour, we can be mentally and emotionally prepared for the spiritual battles we might face. Also, in Philippians 4:6-7, he admonishes, *"Do not be anxious about anything, but in every situation, by prayer and petition, with thanksgiving, present your requests to God. And the peace of God, which transcends all understanding, will guard your hearts and your minds in Christ Jesus."* (*NIV*). This verse encourages us to bring our worries and anxieties to God, trusting in His peace to guard our minds and emotions. He further states in Colossians 3:2, *"Set your minds on things above, not on earthly things."* *(NIV)*. This verse reminds us to focus our minds on God and His kingdom rather than being consumed by the worries and distractions of this world. By applying these and other biblical principles to our lives, we can cultivate a strong and disciplined mind and be mentally and emotionally prepared for the challenges of life.

What are some strategies that can be used to gird up our minds? One of the most important scriptural strategies for girding up the loins of your mind is to renew your mind with the Word of God. Romans 12:2a says, *"Do not conform to the pattern of this world, but be transformed by the renewing of your mind." (NIV)*. This means we should fill our minds with the truth of God's Word and allow it to transform our thinking and attitudes.

An important scriptural strategy for girding up the loins of your mind is to take every thought captive, which means holding it accountable, wrestle with it, and cast it down if it is not lining up with the Word of God.

"Casting down imaginations, and every high thing that exalteth itself against the knowledge of God, and bringing into captivity every thought to the obedience of Christ; and having in a readiness to revenge all disobedience, when your obedience is fulfilled." (2 Corinthians 10:5-6 – KJV).

We do not always think like Christ or the way Christ expects us to think. God's ways are higher than ours, and His thoughts are higher than ours. Many times, we fail to give serious thought and reflection to the things we hear, forgetting that if we fail to do so, it could have serious implications for the future.

Another important scriptural strategy is to pray daily, asking God for wisdom and understanding to navigate life. James 1:5 says, *"If any of you lacks wisdom, you should ask God, who gives generously to all without finding fault, and it will be given to you."* (*NIV*). By praying for wisdom and understanding, we can gain the insights we need to navigate life's challenges and make wise decisions.

Finally, girding up the loins of your mind means guarding your thoughts and emotions. Philippians 4:8 says, *"Finally, brothers and sisters, whatever is true, whatever is noble, whatever is right, whatever is pure, whatever is lovely, whatever is admirable—if anything is excellent or praiseworthy—think about such things."* (*NIV*). *As* we remain focused on positive and uplifting thoughts, we guard our minds against negative and destructive thoughts. Cultivating such spiritual balance anchors our minds and enriches our overall well-being. The scripture provides a compass for our minds, offering clarity and perspective amid the boisterous currents of life. Through spiritual balance, we discover a reservoir of inner strength and resilience to empower us to tackle life's trials with greater level-headedness and a sense of purpose.

We find ourselves in an era filled with numerous challenges and complexities, and to truly value the richness of life, it becomes imperative to establish equilibrium in every facet of our existence. Life is multifaceted, and it demands that we not only address these difficulties but also strive to attain a sense of harmony across all aspects of our lives. The scripture encourages health and wholeness in spirit, soul, and body.

"Beloved, I wish above all things that you prosper and be in health, even as thy soul prospereth." (3 John 1:1-2 – KJV).

In these trying times, achieving balance is the key to unlocking a fulfilling life. This balance extends to various physical, emotional, intellectual, social, and spiritual dimensions. It implies that we need to carefully allocate our time, energy, and attention to each of these areas so that they complement and support one another. Balancing our physical well-being through proper nutrition, exercise, and adequate rest ensures we have the vitality and resilience to face challenges. Emotionally, managing stress, nurturing positive relationships, and cultivating our inner emotional intelligence is important, allowing us to navigate the turbulent waters of life with grace and composure.

Intellectual balance promotes lifelong learning, awareness, and adaptability, keeping us mentally agile in a changing world. The social aspect focuses on building meaningful connections and supporting others, as relationships provide strength and purpose. Spiritual balance encourages introspection, seeking purpose, and understanding our place in the universe, offering grounding and perspective during life's challenges. Together, these elements create a foundation not just for survival but for thriving—enabling a fulfilling and resilient life, even in adversity.

DISCUSSION QUESTIONS

1 Peter 1:13 says you are to *"Gird up the loins of your mind."* What does this metaphor mean in the context of mental health, and how can we apply this principle to protect our minds from negative influences and maintain good mental health?

The Bible often encourages believers to renew their minds (see Romans 12:2) and think on things that are pure and praiseworthy (see Philippians 4:8). How can these teachings help individuals on their journey to maintain good mental health and emotional well-being?

2 Timothy 1:7 states, *"For God hath not given us the spirit of fear; but of power, and of love, and of a sound mind."* *(KJV)*. How can a reliance on faith and a connection with God positively impact our mental health, and what practical steps can individuals take to strengthen their minds in the face of adversity and anxiety?

PRAYER

Dear heavenly Father,

I thank You for the holy scriptures. It serves as a lamp to my feet and a light to my path in this world full of noise and distraction. Dear Lord, please help me to anchor my thoughts in Your truth, causing it to gird up the loins of my mind. Please help me to be vigilant in guarding what I allow to dwell in my heart and mind.

Teach me to fix my thoughts on what is true, noble, right, pure, lovely, and admirable, just as You instruct in Philippians 4:8. When negativity tries to take root, when fear, doubt, or bitterness creep in, remind me of what is excellent and praiseworthy. Help me to choose Your peace over the chaos, and to fill my heart with what reflects Your character.

Father, I surrender my thoughts to You. Please shape them for Your glory.

Amen.

CHAPTER 14

ENCOUNTERS IN THE SECRET PLACE

Experiences of encountering God are profoundly transformative, serving as pivotal junctures in the lives of those who experience them. These encounters not only chart the trajectory of one's existence but also propel the individual toward the fulfilment of their divine purpose and calling.

Speaking of an encounter, I am referring to a significant life-transforming experience or interaction between individuals and God. The Bible is like a beautiful landscape filled with many stories and moments of different people meeting God, and suddenly, there is a dramatic change in their lives and behaviours. I firmly believe that in this current era, the Lord desires His people to have life-changing experiences and encounters, empowering us to positively impact both the present and future generations through God's divine power. These experiences are not just for our benefit but are meant to shape us into vessels of blessings for those around us now and for generations to come. Hence, the call to "come up higher" in Revelation 4:1-2, *"After this I looked, and, behold, a door was opened in heaven: and the first voice which I heard was as it were of a trumpet talking with me; which said, Come up hither, and I will show thee things which must be hereafter. And immediately I was in the spirit: and, behold, a throne was set in heaven, and one sat on the throne." (KJV)*.

Dear reader, my heartfelt prayer is that you may tune your ears to hear the voice of the Father just as Apostle John did. May you move beyond the periphery of religiosity, transcending mere rituals and doctrines, to forge a deeper connection with the eternal, self-existing Father. Let us open our hearts to receive similar spiritual revelations that Apostle John experienced when he was graced with the profound privilege of hearing God's voice. His encounter with God was not confined to religious traditions; it was a direct communion with the Father. John was introduced to the glorified Jesus. It is time for us to move away from formalities and ascend to the hill of the Lord.

To "leave the periphery of religiosity" means to venture beyond the external paraphernalia of religious practice. It entails stepping away from the superficial aspects of religion, which may often involve empty rituals or dogmas devoid of genuine spiritual connection. Instead, it calls for a profound shift towards a more personal and authentic relationship with God. Sadly, many Christians seem to prioritize their church tradition and cultural norms over an authentic, genuine relationship with God. The time has come for us to spend time with God in the secret place; we must imitate the Patriarchs of old who forsook everything to experience more of God. Oh, how the earth is longing and groaning to experience the authenticity of the sons of God operating in the power of the Holy Ghost. Creation knows things about us that we have not yet come into; that understanding or revelation about ourselves. The angels continue to be amazed about us—the born-again, recreated, regenerated species on the earth. Listen to their questions; *"What is man, that thou art mindful of him? And the son of man, that thou visitest him? For thou hast made him a little lower than the angels, and hast crowned him with glory and honour." (Psalm 8:4-5 - KJV).*

Today, I am excited to introduce you to the remarkable life of Moses and the profound encounters that transformed him. I hope that as we explore the depth and significance of his experiences, we will be inspired and encouraged to embark on our own spiritual journeys of transformation. Moses' story is a powerful example of how encounters with God can shape our lives in profound ways, and it invites us to consider the potential for transformation in our spiritual walk.

Moses, born to the Levite couple, Amram and Jochebed, was a significant figure in biblical history. His lineage is traced back to the great patriarch, Abraham, making him part of the heritage of the tribe of Levi. This ancestry connects Moses to a rich legacy of faith and tradition, which played a pivotal role in shaping his life and mission.

During the time of Moses' birth, the people of God were enduring severe hardships. This was due to a decree issued by Pharaoh who ordered the killing of all baby boys to annihilate the people of God. However, it is important to note that God was steadfastly on the side of His people, watching over them and preserving their survival despite these oppressive circumstances.

Moses' life was characterized by miraculous, powerful, and life-transforming events, starting with his decision to leave the wealthy lifestyle of Egypt to embrace his calling.

"Choosing rather to suffer affliction with the people of God, than to enjoy the pleasures of sin for a season, esteeming the reproach of Christ greater riches than the treasures in Egypt: for he had respect unto the recompense of the reward." (Hebrews 11:25-26 –KJV).

This decision marked the beginning of a profound transformation in Moses' life, where he left behind the allure of worldly comforts and embraced a path of spiritual growth and purpose.

Today, we are called upon to make a similar decision and commitment if we aspire to make a meaningful impact on our world and leave a positive legacy for the generations that follow us. Just as Moses chose to separate himself from the worldly enticements of Egypt to fulfil a divine calling, we too are encouraged to detach from distractions and embrace a higher purpose if we wish to leave a lasting mark on our society and inspire those who come after us. Each one of us should seek a personal encounter with God, allowing ourselves to be touched by the consuming fire of the Holy Spirit. This divine encounter can strip away the worldly layers we often wear, revealing our true selves in the light of God's presence. In this spiritual refinement, we can find deeper meaning and purpose in our lives.

THE BURNING BUSH

"Now Moses kept the flock of Jethro his father-in-law, the priest of Midian: and he led the flock to the backside of the desert, and came to the mountain of God, even to Horeb. And the angel of the Lord appeared unto him in a flame of fire out of the midst of a bush: and he looked, and, behold, the bush burned with fire, and the bush was not consumed. And Moses said, I will now turn aside, and see this great sight, why the bush is not burnt. And when the Lord saw that he turned aside to see, God called unto him out of the midst of the bush, and said, Moses, Moses. And he said, here am I, And he said, Draw not nigh hither: put off thy shoes from off thy feet, for the place whereon thou standest is holy ground." (Exodus 3:1-5 – KJV).

Even though the Bible does not explicitly mention that Moses removed his physical sandals during the subsequent conversation, it is reasonable to infer that he likely did so. This assumption is grounded in the reverence and respect commonly shown in the presence of the divine, where removing one's footwear can symbolize humility and recognition of the sacredness of the encounter.

I propose that when Moses removed his sandals before God, it symbolized more than a physical act—it represented leaving behind his old life. In that moment, he shed his past identity, fears, and self-reliance to embrace God's calling. This act of surrender marked the start of a transformative journey, reminding us that encountering God often requires letting go of the familiar to step into His purpose.

For nearly four decades, he had been essentially "doing his own thing," tending to his father-in-law's flock, fulfilling his role as a husband, and living a relatively ordinary life. However, at this moment, it became clear to him that his spiritual journey demanded a different kind of "spiritual sandals." It was a call to step into a new and profound purpose that would guide him on a path filled with divine significance.

"And the Lord said, I have surely seen the affliction of my people which are in Egypt, and have heard their cry by reason of their taskmasters; for I know their sorrows; And I am come down to deliver them out of the hand of the Egyptians, and to bring them up out of that land unto a good land and a large, unto a land flowing with milk and honey; unto the place of the Canaanites, and the Hittites, and the Amorites, and the Perizzites, and the Hivites, and the Jebusites. Now therefore, behold, the cry of the children of Israel is come unto me: and I have also seen the oppression

wherewith the Egyptians oppress them. Come now therefore, and I will send thee unto Pharaoh, that thou mayest bring forth my people the children of Israel out of Egypt. And Moses said unto God, who am I, that I should go unto Pharaoh, and that I should bring forth the children of Israel out of Egypt?" (Exodus 3:7-11 – KJV).

As you immerse yourself in this narrative, I invite you to pause and reflect on the journey ahead of you. Think about the paths you are yet to walk, the challenges you may face, and the opportunities that await your discovery. Each step ahead holds the potential for learning, growth, and development. Be aware that every experience, whether joyful or difficult, has significance. Just as Moses embarked on a transformative path when he encountered God, there may be new and profound encounters in your own life that will shape your spiritual journey and lead you to unforeseen opportunities and revelations.

"For we know that the whole creation groaneth and travaileth in pain together until now. And not only they, but ourselves also, which have the first fruits of the Spirit, even we ourselves groan within ourselves, waiting for the adoption, to wit, the redemption of our body." (Romans 8:22-23 – KJV).

SUMMARY

Exodus 3:3 says, *"And Moses said, I will now turn aside, and see this great sight, why the bush is not burnt." (KJV).*

This encounter with the burning bush left an indelible impression on Moses, a vivid memory that would shape the course of his existence. Despite his initial reservations and a keen awareness of his own limitations, Moses found himself compelled to heed God's call and carry out the mission entrusted to him. This was no casual meeting; this was a response to the groan (creation) of the children of Israel in Egyptian bondage, and a covenant between them and God is at stake because a deliverer is needed. Despite the demanding responsibilities of tending his flock, I propose that Moses managed to carve out precious moments to encounter God at the sacred Mount Horeb.

Moses showed remarkable commitment to nurturing his spiritual connection with God during his daily duties as a shepherd. He made a deliberate choice to create opportunities for communion with God on Mount Horeb, a place of profound significance in his spiritual journey.

In essence, Moses' ability to meet with God while attending to his flock is a testament to his dedication to his earthly responsibilities and spiritual calling. It serves as a powerful reminder of the importance of finding moments of divine connection amidst life's demands and responsibilities, highlighting the profound impact such encounters can have on one's life and purpose. Notice how he left his sheep and journeyed to Horeb, often called the mountain of God. Moses set aside his responsibilities as a shepherd to seek God. We too should be open to moments of spiritual connection that can enrich our journey and bring us closer to

God, whether through planned times of prayer and reflection or through unexpected experiences that lead us to encounter God in profound ways.

Observing Moses' journey over the next four decades, we see the extraordinary successes in the service of God, including leading the Israelites out of slavery in Egypt, receiving the Ten Commandments on Mount Sinai, and guiding the people through the wilderness. His commitment and leadership during this time were undoubtedly influenced by his profound encounter with the burning bush, which set him on a course to do great things for God and His people.

DISCUSSION QUESTIONS

What lessons can we draw from Moses' initial hesitation and doubt when he was called by God at the burning bush?

How can we apply these lessons to overcome our own doubts and fears when God calls us to specific tasks or missions in our Christian walk?

In what ways did Moses' initial reluctance and doubts during his encounter with the burning bush resonate with common challenges believers face when confronted with God's call? How can we overcome similar doubts and fears when we sense God leading us in specific directions in our lives?

Moses' encounter with the burning bush ultimately led to a profound transformation in his life and a divine mission. How can we discern between ordinary experiences and genuine encounters with God in our Christian walk? What signs or characteristics should we look for to identify God's calling and direction for our lives?

PRAYER

Father, I come before You with a heart humbled by the weight of Your calling. Just as Moses turned aside to behold the burning bush, help me to pause amidst the noise of my daily life and recognise the sacred moments when You are near. Please soften my heart to respond when You speak.

Lord, I know I am limited, flawed, and often hesitant—just like Moses. Yet, You still choose to call and use those who feel unworthy. Father, please remind me that it is not about my ability but Your presence and power working through me. Lord, give me the courage to say yes, even when I feel unsure, because there is a world groaning for deliverance, and You are faithful to Your people. Thank You, Father, for being the God who sees, the God who hears, and the God who remembers His people.

Please use me, Lord, in whatever way You choose so Your glory can manifest through me.

Amen.

CHAPTER 15

A RADICAL CHANGE

Before Saul was radically converted, he was depicted as a figure marked by cruelty and a seeming lack of compassion; he was known for his zealous persecution of the early Christians. His transformation was not merely a change of heart but a profound revelation of God's love, which compelled him to turn away from his former life and embrace a new path dedicated to Christ. In his own words, he wrote, *"... Forgetting those things which are behind, and reaching forth unto the things which are before, I press towards the mark for the prize of the high calling of God in Christ Jesus." (Philippians 3:13-14 - KJV).*

This transformation from Saul, the persecutor, to Paul, the passionate Apostle of Jesus Christ, exemplifies the redemptive power of faith and God's capacity to radically change the course of a person's life. Saul's journey reminds us that even those who may seem beyond redemption can experience a profound conversion and become instruments of God's grace, offering hope and salvation to others.

THE DAMASCUS ROAD EXPERIENCE

"And as he journeyed, he came near Damascus: and suddenly there shined round about him a light from heaven: And he fell to the earth, and heard a voice saying unto him, Saul, Saul, why persecutest thou me? And he said, who art thou, Lord? And the Lord said I am Jesus whom thou persecutest: it is hard for thee to kick against the pricks. And he trembling and astonished said, Lord, what wilt thou have me to do? And the Lord said unto him, Arise, and go into the city, and it shall be told thee what thou must do." (Acts 9:3-6 – KJV).

CLARIFICATION/SPIRITUAL REVELATION

"But the Lord said unto him, go thy way: for he is a chosen vessel unto me, to bear my name before the Gentiles, and kings, and the children of Israel: For I will show him how great things he must suffer for my name's sake. And Ananias went his way, and entered into the house; and putting his hands on him said, Brother Saul, the Lord, even Jesus, that appeared unto thee in the way as thou camest, hath sent me, that thou mightiest receive thy sight, and be filled with the Holy Ghost." (Acts 9:15-17 – KJV).

SEPARATION

"But when it pleased God, who separated me from my mother's womb, and called me by his grace, to reveal his Son in me, that I might preach Him among the heathen; immediately I conferred not with flesh and blood: Neither
138

went I up to Jerusalem to them which were apostles before me; but I went into Arabia, and returned again unto Damascus." (Galatians 1:15-17 - KJV).

This text highlights the sovereignty of God in calling and setting apart individuals for His purposes. Paul acknowledges that his calling was not an afterthought or a result of his own merit but was part of God's divine plan even before he was born. This is a reminder to us who are believers in Christ that God has a unique purpose for each of us, ordained before we took our first breath. Being "separated" means being chosen, consecrated, and set apart for God's work. It is a call to live a life of holiness and dedication to Him.

"And called me by his grace."

Apostle Paul emphasizes that his calling was entirely by God's grace, not by his own works or worthiness. This is a humbling truth for all believers to appreciate, that our calling and ability to serve God are gifts of His grace, not something we earn. With this in mind, we will not rely on our own strength or qualifications but on God's unmerited favour and empowerment.

"To reveal His Son in me."

The ultimate purpose of Paul's calling was for Christ to be revealed in him. This means Paul's life was to become a living testimony of Jesus—His love, power, and truth. For

139

believers today, this is a call to let Christ be seen in our lives. It is about allowing the character, teachings, and mission of Jesus to shape our thoughts, actions, and relationships.

"That I might preach Him among the heathen."

Paul's specific mission was to preach the gospel to the Gentiles (the "heathen"). This shows that God's call often includes a specific audience or mission. We need to be mindful that our calling may involve reaching specific people or communities, which might challenge us to step out of our comfort zones and share the gospel with those who do not yet know Christ.

"Immediately I conferred not with flesh and blood."

After his encounter with Christ, Paul did not seek human approval or validation. He recognized that his calling was divine and did not depend on human endorsement. This teaches believers to prioritize God's direction over human opinions. We must act in faith when God calls us, even if others do not understand or support us.

"Neither went I up to Jerusalem to them which were apostles before me; but I went into Arabia, and returned again unto Damascus."

Apostle Paul did not immediately seek out the established apostles in Jerusalem. Instead, he spent time in Arabia, likely in solitude and preparation, before returning to

Damascus. This highlights the importance of seasons of preparation and intimacy with God before stepping into public ministry. For believers, it is a reminder that God often calls us to periods of waiting, learning, and spiritual growth before fully launching us into our assignments. Paul's life is a powerful example of how a divine calling, rooted in grace and marked by obedience, can transform an individual and impact the world for Christ. As believers, we are invited to walk in this same spirit of surrender, allowing God to reveal His Son in us and use us for His glory.

SUMMARY

When Paul received his divine calling, he found himself at a crossroads where he had to make a decisive choice. He recognized that to truly fulfil the mission set before him, he needed to break free from the familiar customs and philosophies prevalent in the society of his day. This meant separating himself from the prevailing human traditions and belief systems that might have hindered his understanding of God's truth.

Paul's decision to distance himself from human traditions and philosophies was not a rejection of wisdom or knowledge but a recognition that the true depths of spiritual understanding and revelation could only be found through seeking God's guidance. It was a deliberate step towards a more profound and direct connection with God.

In this pursuit, Paul was committed to uncovering the mysteries of God and the gospel of Jesus Christ. His life's purpose became centered on receiving and sharing the revelations granted to him through his faith and relationship with God. This included profound theological insights and a deep understanding of God's plan for salvation, all of which he passionately conveyed in his letters and teachings.

Paul's call to ministry and his decision to separate himself from the constraints of human traditions serve as an inspiration for believers today. It encourages us to prioritize our spiritual journey and seek divine revelations amidst the noise and distractions of the world. It underscores the importance of a deep and personal connection with God, where we can uncover profound truths and insights that can transform our lives and the lives of those around us.

Believers are called into a place of divine intimacy and communion into the secret place. We will be able to effectively impact our generation and successive generations. Therefore, let us consciously set ourselves apart to spend quality time with the Lord as Apostle Paul, Moses, Apostle John, and others did.

DISCUSSION QUESTIONS

Paul's conversion on the road to Damascus was a dramatic and life-changing event. How can modern believers draw inspiration from his transformation to navigate their own spiritual journeys and seek a deeper connection with God?

In Paul's conversion story, the encounter with the risen Christ led to a complete reorientation of his life and beliefs. How can we apply the principles of radical transformation and surrender to our own lives, especially in the face of challenges and doubts?

Paul's conversion not only changed him personally but also had a profound impact on the early Christian church and the spread of Christianity. How can we, as individuals and as a community, leverage our own spiritual experiences and transformations to positively influence the world and further the message of Christ?

PRAYER

Heavenly Father,
We come before You, inspired by the dramatic transformation of Paul on the road to Damascus. Just as You radically reoriented his life, we ask for a fresh encounter with the risen Christ in our own spiritual journeys. Open our eyes to see You more clearly, soften our hearts to hear Your voice, and give us the courage to surrender completely to Your will. May Paul's story remind us that no one is beyond the reach of Your grace, and You can transform even the hardest of hearts for Your glory.

Lord, in moments of doubt, fear, or challenge, please help us embrace the principles of radical transformation and surrender that Paul exemplified. Teach us to lay down our own plans, pride, and preconceptions, trusting that Your ways are higher and Your purposes are perfect. Please strengthen our faith to believe that You can use our brokenness, struggles, and past to bring about Your divine plan.

Father, we pray for the courage and boldness to let our own spiritual transformations impact the world around us. Just as Paul's conversion fuelled the growth of the early church, may our encounters with You ignite a passion to share Your love and truth with others. Help us, as individuals and as a community, to be vessels of Your grace, instruments of Your peace, and messengers of Your hope. Empower us to live in such a way that our lives point others to Christ and further the message of Your kingdom.

Thank You, Lord, for the example of Paul and for the reminder that no transformation is too great for Your power. May we continually seek a deeper connection with You, trusting that You are always at work in us and through us. In Jesus' name we pray. Amen.

CHAPTER 16

MY JOURNEY INTO THE SECRET PLACE

It started with an encounter I had with the Lord in 1993 while working in the Cayman Islands. During an open vision, I witnessed a vivid scene where I stood next to my deceased grandfather, who had passed away due to old age when I was just six years old. The clarity of this vision was astonishing, especially since I was not living in my homeland but was in a foreign land. I was deep in prayer and intercession during that time, seeking answers and solutions to my problems. Suddenly, I experienced a remarkable shift, as if I had been transported to my place of birth, Main Ridge, in the Parish of Clarendon, Jamaica. In this new location, it felt as though I had a divine purpose to fulfil and engage in a significant spiritual transaction with the Lord because there were scenes from my past that haunted me. My upbringing unfolded as that of an only child, marked by the abandonment and rejection of my mother, who entrusted my care to my grandparents. While this experience held its challenges, my grandparents provided me with an abundance of love and care. Regrettably, I have only fleeting memories of my grandmother, as she passed away when I was a mere three or four years old. Despite my limited recollections of her, the warm and nurturing environment she created during my early years lingers.

My grandfather provided me with care and affection, doing his utmost to shield and lead me down the right path. However, after his death, everything changed, and it felt as though my life ended. I started to experience physical, emotional, mental, and sexual abuse from persons who I thought should have nurtured and cared for me, but instead, the enemy used them to hurt me. This opened the door for promiscuity, rebellion, hatred, and bitterness. As I observed the scene of a young girl—myself—weeping beside my grandfather's lifeless body, I distinctly heard the Holy Spirit whisper, *"When he departed, a part of you also departed."* This served as a revelation to me, given that I had matured into a married woman with a family of my own. However, I grappled with difficulties in cultivating healthy interpersonal relationships.

I found it challenging to place trust in others, and I became increasingly cautious about individuals seeking friendship. Even when it came to surrendering my entire life to the Lord, I hesitated because I loved myself and felt like I had to protect myself from being hurt. As the vision persisted, my heart shattered, and I found myself sobbing uncontrollably. Once more, the gentle voice of the Lord softly uttered, *"Give Me all of you."* It was the most affectionate, nurturing, and reassuring voice I had ever encountered, so without hesitation, I wholeheartedly surrendered to the Lord.

In addition to enlightening my understanding of the Word, the Holy Spirit has proven to be an invaluable guide throughout my journey. My deep yearning for a closer connection with God intensified, sparking a profound transformation in the way I engaged with scripture. I found myself drawn into a more intimate interaction with the Word of God. As this hunger for a deeper relationship with the Lord grew within me, my approach to scripture underwent a remarkable change. Instead of merely reading the texts, I began to immerse myself in them, seeking not only knowledge but a profound spiritual connection. The pages of the Bible became a gateway to encountering God on a personal level.

Each passage, verse, and story became a vessel through which I communed with God. I no longer approached scripture as a distant observer but as an active participant in the ongoing dialogue between God and His people. It was as if the words themselves came alive, resonating with new meaning and relevance. Through this heightened interaction with scripture, I discovered hidden treasures of wisdom, guidance, and comfort that had previously eluded me. The Bible transformed from a mere book into a sacred conduit, bridging the gap between my heart and the heart of God.

This intensified hunger for God and the deepening intimacy with scripture became a source of spiritual nourishment and renewal. It fuelled my desire to grow in faith, drawing me closer to the One who had inspired these sacred words. In this journey, I found that my heart echoed the words of the Psalmist: *"As the deer pants for streams of water, so my soul pants for you, my God." (Psalm 42:1 - NIV).*

The Holy Spirit has grown remarkably real and precious to me since that initial encounter. He has been an intimate guide who introduced me to the profound depths of the Father's heart, brimming with love, compassion, and boundless mercy. His presence has illuminated the scriptures, unveiling hidden treasures of wisdom and a source of strength during challenging moments. He assists me in making difficult decisions, offering guidance and peace in the midst of uncertainty. Particularly during life's most daunting trials, such as confronting serious illnesses and the prospect of death, His grace became my anchor. Through His comforting presence, I find the courage to navigate these trying circumstances with resilience and faith.

PRAYER

Dear heavenly Father,
Today, my heart is overflowing with gratitude for all Your blessings. Thank You for stirring within me a deep yearning to know You more. Daddy, what began as a quiet longing has grown into a life-changing transformation, and I give You all the glory.

Thank You for awakening my heart to the beauty and power of Your Word. So, I no longer approach scripture as a distant observer but as one who is welcomed into an intimate conversation with You. Each verse, each passage has become a sacred encounter—a doorway into Your presence.

Lord, I am in awe of how You meet me within the pages of the Bible, how the words come alive with meaning, alive with Your Spirit. Thank You for revealing hidden treasures, for guiding me, comforting me, and speaking directly to the depths of my soul.

I thank You for the Holy Spirit, my constant companion and teacher, who has gently led me into the very heart of the Father—where I have discovered love beyond measure, compassion beyond comprehension, and mercy that knows no bounds.

This deepened hunger for You, Lord, has become my sustenance. As the deer pants for streams of water, so my soul thirsts for You. You have become my joy, strength, peace, and portion forever.

Thank You for this sacred journey. Please help me continue to draw closer to You each day; cause me to remain rooted in Your truth, nourished by Your presence, and transformed by Your love.

Amen.

CONCLUSION

SUMMARY OF THE SECRET PLACE

This summary explores the biblical foundations and theological significance of the secret place. It refers to a unique and intimate space of communion between individuals and God in Psalm 91:1. The Psalmist lays a foundational scriptural basis for the secret place: *"He that dwelleth in the secret place of the most High shall abide under the shadow of the Almighty." (KJV)*. Here, the secret place is depicted as a dwelling where one finds shelter and protection in the presence of God.

In Matthew 6:6, Jesus emphasizes the importance of the secret place in prayer: *"But thou, when thou prayest, enter into thy closet, and when thou hast shut thy door, pray to thy Father which is in secret; and thy Father which seeth in secret shall reward thee openly." (KJV)*. This verse underscores the private and intimate nature of communication with God.

In Exodus 33:11, the story of Moses is another biblical example. *"And the Lord spake unto Moses face to face, as a man speaketh unto his friend. And he turned again into the camp: but his servant Joshua, the son of Nun, a young man, departed not out of the tabernacle." (KJV).* Moses met God in the "tent of meeting," a designated place for intimate encounters with God. Also, he spent quality time in the secret place—a place of deep communion and divine encounter. As he lingered in God's presence, something extraordinary happened: his face began to shine with the glory of God, reflecting the divine brilliance and majesty he had been exposed to. The radiance was so overwhelming that he had to place a veil over his face just to interact with the Israelites, whose lives were not yet attuned to such holy intimacy. This teaches us a powerful truth—those who dwell in God's presence carry a visible mark of His glory, one that sets them apart.

David, known as a man after God's own heart, understood the value of this closeness. His deepest longing was not for earthly success, riches, or even victory over his enemies—it was to live continually in God's presence. In Psalm 27:4, he declared, *"One thing I have desired of the Lord, that will I seek after: that I may dwell in the house of the Lord all the days of my life." (KJV).* For David, nearness to God was not just an occasional retreat; it was his greatest pursuit. Additionally, we observe the pattern of Jesus that, despite His demanding ministry, He frequently withdrew to solitary places to pray and reconnect with His Father in the secret place. These moments of prayer were not just a spiritual discipline—they were the source of His power, wisdom, and unshakable peace. So then, if the Son of God needed such intimate fellowship with the Father, how much more do we?

The secret place promotes an environment of privacy where individuals can be authentic before God. In this sacred space, there is no need for pretense or a religious performance, such as only reading our favourite Psalm or singing our favourite songs, which are commendable. But I tell you that a lifestyle of unbroken communion with the Holy Spirit is better and should be our daily pursuit. Moses' radiant face, David's hungry heart, and Jesus' solitary prayers all reveal that those who live in the secret place aren't just spiritually enriched—they are eternally shielded, empowered, and transformed. The secret place is conducive to divine revelation; the scripture speaks of men and women who received divine revelations and insights in this realm.

The secret place is a personal retreat and a source of empowerment for effective ministry. Biblical leaders like Paul, John, and Moses were fortified and empowered through their secret encounters with God, enabling them to impact their generations significantly. Conversely, those who cultivate a deep relationship with God in this manner leave behind a spiritual legacy that can influence successive generations.

Additionally, we see in the life of Abraham that a close and lasting relationship was cultivated over a period of time. God calls him "friend" (see James 2:23). Hence, when he was asked to offer up his son, Isaac, as a sacrifice unto God, he did not hesitate. This act of obedience was an expression of his love, devotion, and an act of worship unto God.

I have personally experienced the profound blessings of dwelling in the secret place of God's presence, and this has revolutionised my entire life. My prayer time and devotional life have taken on a new perspective. I have found a sense of fulfilment and joy in my everyday life that I had never known before.

One of the most remarkable changes I have observed within myself is in the area of human and interpersonal relationships. The complexities and emotional challenges that once weighed heavily on me no longer have the same power. Instead, I now possess a newfound ability to appreciate everyone who crosses my path, embracing their unique personalities and perspectives. Interestingly, despite being abandoned by my mother and never having met her in person, my heart has been touched by a profound love for her. I find myself regularly lifting her in prayer, earnestly hoping that God will encounter her on her journey through life, just as He has graciously touched mine.

This transformation within me serves as a testament to the incredible impact of seeking refuge in a secret place with God. It has not only enriched my relationship with the Lord but has also opened my heart to express love and forgiveness to everyone. Moreover, as a mother of three grown children and wife for over forty-one years to the same person, I am living a life filled with gratitude, love, and a deep sense of purpose. This happened because of the transformative work of the Holy Spirit.

DISCUSSION QUESTIONS

How has seeking refuge in the secret place for a deeper spiritual connection with God helped you find resilience in the face of life's challenges? Share specific experiences and insights from your journey.

What practical steps or habits have you incorporated into your life to create and maintain a secret place where you can regularly commune with God? How has this practice impacted your ability to face adversity and make meaningful decisions?

How can the concept of the secret place, as discussed in the context of seeking God's presence and guidance, be applied to support others who are struggling with life's challenges? What role can faith and spiritual practices play in helping individuals find solace and strength during difficult times?

PRAYER

Heavenly Father,
I come before You with a heart full of gratitude for the refuge of the secret place where I have encountered Your presence in the most intimate and life-changing ways. Thank You for drawing me close, revealing Your heart to me, and transforming my life through the power of Your love. In this

hidden place, I have found renewal, strength, and a deeper understanding of who You are and who I am in You.

Lord, I thank You for the profound work You have done in my heart, teaching me to love unconditionally, even those who have caused me pain. I lift up my mother to You, asking that Your grace would meet her wherever she is. Touch her life, Lord, and draw her into the same intimate relationship with You that has become my greatest treasure. May she experience Your love, forgiveness, and redemption in a way that transforms her heart and life.

As a wife, mother, and friend, I ask that You use me to leave a lasting spiritual legacy for my family and those around me. May my life be a testament to Your faithfulness, love, and transformative power. Help me to reflect Your heart in all that I do and to pour out the blessings I have received in the secret place into the lives of others.

I commit my life afresh to seeking You above all else, trusting that You will continue to lead me, shape me, and use me for your glory. In Jesus' precious name, I pray.

Amen.

www.ingramcontent.com/pod-product-compliance
Lightning Source LLC
LaVergne TN
LVHW051239080426

835513LV00016B/1676